International Environment Management

International Environment Management

Dr. P. Rathnaswamy

Foreword by
Hans-C von Sponeck
UN Resident Coordinator

1998

MANAS PUBLICATIONS

NEW DELHI-110 002

MANAS PUBLICATIONS
(Publishers, Distributors & Exporters)
4819/XI, Varun House, Mathur Lane,
24, Ansari Road, Darya Ganj,
New Delhi-110002 (INDIA)
Ph.: 3260783, 3265523, 2919762
Fax : 011 - 3272766 & 2927854
E-Mail : manas.vkgarg@axcess.net.in

ISBN 81-7049-091-X

First Published 1998

Typeset at
Innovative Processors,
New Delhi-110 002

Printed in India at
Santosh Offset, Delhi,
and Published by Mrs. Suman Lata for
Manas Publications, 4819/XI, Varun House,
Mathur Lane, 24, Ansari Road, Darya Ganj,
New Delhi-110002 (INDIA)

UNITED NATIONS **NATIONS UNIES**

FOREWORD

United Nations World Conferences are major events in their own right. However benefits do not come just from the specific conference itself, but from preparing for such meetings and moving forward after the event to achieve established goals and commitments.

The UN Conference for Environment and Development held in Rio de Janeiro in 1992 produced a major plan of action in the shape of AGENDA 21, a comprehensive enumeration of what different actors in society need to do if we are to sustain the environment and natural resources on which people depend.

Five years after Rio, the world community is meeting once again in the same city to take stock of how much has been accomplished in this regard. Unfortunately, even the most ebullient optimist will have to accept that much more remains unaddressed than has been achieved. One of the reasons for this situation is undoubtedly the lack of comprehensive action and, most importantly, the only too often absence of political will. The other is the paucity of many sufficiently specialised studies on specific topics which are in the public domain and provide easily implementable working guidelines for institutions.

Dr.Ratnaswamy's book on "International Environment Management" is a welcome contribution in this context. As an international civil servant I am naturally encouraged by his conclusion that world cooperation through international organisations under United Nations leadership remains the principal engine for sustainable development.

Hans-C von Sponeck
UN Resident Coordinator

Preface

Global Environment degradation is another conflicting area where the concept of development is challenged. The developing nations have not achieved development sufficiently and they are subjected to poverty and malnutrition. With the result there is a persistent challenge to development on the one hand and environment on the other.

The Stockholm Conference 1972 has initiated the arguments for making development and environment achievable. In the process, the efforts have been made to identify the areas in which the development and environment have been increasingly contradictory to each other. Having understood the contradictions the role of International Environmental Law was recognized for the first time formally while reviewing the performance of International Environmental Agreements and Treaties. The Stockholm Conference has also recognized the need and necessity of international action and cooperation through International institutions and organisations so as to pursue and incorporate national attitudes towards environment and development for an acceptable and comprehensive global policies that may be implemented.

In the last twenty-six years there has been growth in international environmental agreements and treaties; there have been changes in global policies towards the environment and development which have successfully developed into a concept of sustainable development; there has been tremendous pressure on international institutions, regional organisations and national institutions; there has been a great demand for pollution-free environment; there have been innumerable policy decisions towards a safer environment and development and there have been successes and failures. The 1992 Earth Summit has given a number of comprehensive policy approaches towards International Environment Management. To achieve International Environment Management different strategies have been successfully discussed and deliberated.

The collective wisdom permits humankind to be rational and judicious and it also influences them to save mankind not only the present but future generations as well. This reflects the concept of sustainable development. International environmental law and international organisations should promote the sustainable development. International environmental law provides a legal framework, norms and procedures to enforce international environmental obligations which are enumerated in international environmental agreements. The growth of international environmental law has instilled more confidence in the minds of the negotiating nations while incorporating the characteristic principles of sustainable development such as the polluter pays principle, the principle of common but discriminated responsibility, the principle of inter-generational equity, etc. Public international law may find these principles beyond the normal scope of equity and enforceability as these do not meet the ordinary legal jurisprudence. International organisations while promoting international cooperation towards sustainable development have developed these principles which are constantly invoked and practised. Resultantly these principles are widely accepted in national law and international law. To promote sustainable development, international environmental law and international organisations are complementary to each other.

The book is divided into the following eight chapters:

1. International Environment Management : An Introduction
2. Conflicts and Controversies: Sustainable Development
3. Problems of Compliance

4. General Principles of International Environmental Law
5. International Environmental Agreements
6. International Organisations
7. Enforcement and Participation
8. Conclusion-Empowerment of Sustainable Development

The first chapter "International Environment Management: An Introduction" deals with issues and need for International Environmental Management. Global issues on environmental degradation and development approaches are discussed in this chapter.

The second chapter on "Conflicts and Controversies: Sustainable Development" briefly discusses that conflicts and controversies are bound to exist and consistent efforts are essential to remove them while promoting sustainable development. There is no one time solution as the concept of sustainable development is dynamic. In order to have a comprehensive view on sustainable development, a historical development on the evolution of the concept of sustainable development, definitions on sustainable development, approaches to sustainable development, and conflicts and controversies of sustainable development are elaborately discussed in this chapter.

The third chapter deals with the problems of compliance and a sketch of the prepared work is also discussed here.

The various principles that are adopted for International Environmental Law like polluter pays principle, the principle of common but discriminated responsibility, the principle of inter-generational equity and so on are discussed to meet its requirements. It explains the principles that are essential to International Environmental Law. These aspects are discussed in the fourth chapter on "General Principles of International Environmental Law".

The fifth chapter on "International Environmental Agreements" narrates the nature, kinds and parties to International

Environmental Agreements. The importance of negotiations and participation in the International Environmental Agreements have also been briefly discussed.

The importance and role of international organisations towards sustainable development are briefly discussed in this chapter. There are so many international institutions which are promoting environment and development. These international organisations include different organs of United Nations and non-governmental organisations. Apart from them there are regional organisations which equally promote environment and development.

The sixth chapter on "Enforcement and Participation" briefly discusses the importance of enforcement of international environmental obligations through international organisations and international cooperation of community of nations with effective participation. It also discusses the problems and consequences with reference to enforcement of environmental obligations and their participation. The problems of compliance of International Environmental Agreements and their participation for enforcement of international environmental obligations are discussed with the help of graphs and diagrams. While discussing them graphically, Carlise Ford Runge's concepts of superior and inferior equilibrium have been adopted but subsequently these explanations have been reorganised and modified. In the process of it new graphical illustrations are developed to project concrete explanations to identify the reasons for non-compliance and non-implementation of International Environmental Agreements.

The concluding chapter briefly discusses the suggestions and recommendations to strengthen enforcement and participation and it is explained through a new theory of "Empowerment of Sustainable Development". The importance of the book is highlighted as under:

— This is one of the pioneering works that discusses the issues and need for International Environment Management.

— This book has undertaken the tasks of identifying problems, conflicts and controversies of sustainable development objectively and attempted to find most acceptable solutions as a humble beginning in the International Environmental Management.

— In this book a new theory of "Empowerment of Sustainable Development" is developed to solve the problem of environment and development. In the process the problems between North and South are convincingly identified and objectively proved that these problems can be resolved through objective means and policies.

— International cooperation can be developed within the competence of United Nations, and International Environmental Agreements can be enforced without sanctions but through active participation by all the nations irrespective of nations belonging to North or South.

— This book establishes that international cooperation can be achieved through international organisations, and UNO is the principal instrument to organise, negotiate, participate, implement and to enforce the concept of sustainable development. This is the most ideal and acceptable way to achieve.

The important achievement of this book demonstrates that international cooperation through international organisations under the leadership of UNO is the solution to achieve sustainable development and not merely by sanctions.

P. Rathnaswamy

Contents

CHAPTER 1

International Environment Management: An Introduction

International environment management is an integral part of global development and it is recognised since the 1972 Stockholm Conference. As there is no single definition on global development it is very difficult to have definite principles of international environment management. The then Secretary General of UNO presented a document on 'Development' in 1994. However, it has not established substantive principles of global development. Many definitions of 'Development' have multiplied the approaches to development. With the result, it has become very difficult to find a common and universally accepted definition of 'Development'. Moreover, neither development theories nor modern theories of development could advocate a comprehensive model of development. The collapse of Soviet Union and Eastern bloc of nations has presented a dilemma to development theories. Growing global environmental degradation has demanded the global attention at various conferences and forums. Growing poverty and malnutrition have also thrown challenges to humanity and community of nations. Development and Environment have apparently turned to be either side of a single coin of humanity. The emergence of third world countries like the South East Asian nations and China has ridiculed the relevance of post-modernity of development. Nevertheless each approach to development has established certain principles and these principles have undergone modifications and at times a drastic change substantially in course of time. It seems that it is difficult to adhere to specific principles constantly always.

Each nation has adopted certain principles historically. India has accepted mixed economy after independence. Yet, there have been modifications. Economic policies are modified when the governments are changed as per their election manifestos. India, in each five year plan, has altered its priorities. In 1990s liberalisation has come in a big way and it continues despite of change in government. It adopted a 'Socialist pattern of Society' at Avadi Conference in 1956 and accordingly, the priorities and industrial policies were framed. Efforts are made to achieve social and economic justice so as to narrow down the poverty. Population below poverty line has been brought down. India could emerge one of the ten industrialised economies with maximum number of scientists and technicians. India has achieved self-sufficiency in food production. India is one of the nations where there is the largest population living below poverty line and suffering from illiteracy in the world. Incidence of poverty in 1985 was 55 per cent and it is expected to be 25.4 per cent in 2000 A.D. Similarly the number of poor was 525 million in 1985 and it is expected to be reduced to 365 million in 2000 A.D.

It is interesting to note that the GDI (Gross Domestic Investment) continued to grow 17.2 per cent in 1963-73, 21.3 per cent in 1973-80, and 24 per cent in 1980-88. Until recently FDI was considered only an extension of colonialism. Today FDI is accepted as one of the sources of investment. Hence, the principles and approaches to development do not remain always the same.

China criticised the economic policies of the Soviet Union. It condemned those policies as part of petty capitalism. In early years, the economic policies of the Soviet Union were considered to be a model to developing nations. The Soviet economy was considered to be a model to sick economies to recover after world wars. Socialism was considered as an alternative to capitalism. Today it is reported that poverty has increased, unemployment has increased, malnutrition is the problem and infant mortality rate is high. Today economic policies are reversed. China has entered into market economy since 1980 even though socialism is the main slogan of economic doctrine. The incidence of poverty was 20 per cent in 1985 and it is projected to be 2.9 per cent in 2000 AD. The number of poor population was 210 million in 1985 and it is projected that such population will be only 209 million in 2000 AD.

Indonesia is a country which has the blend of military rule and it has achieved higher growth rate of GDI—15.8 per cent in 1965-73, 24.5 per cent in 1973-80, and 27.6 per cent in 1980-88. Similarly, it has achieved a higher growth rate of Gross National Savings—13.7 per cent in 1965-73, 24.6 per cent in 1973-80 and 24.4 per cent in 1980-88. Similarly there is higher growth rate in the case of South Korea which has opened its economy for FDI and free enterprise. It has accepted market economy like Singapore and Taiwan. Japan was a shattered economy in early 1950s. Today Japan is an economic super power. With recovery of economy after 1920s and world wars, the United States has advocated protectionism more vehemently than ever before. After Second World Wars, the United States pleaded for free world trade while Britain and America were discussing the world trading system like GATT, etc. Thatcherism had reversed certain basic economic principles in 1980s and 1990s. The pattern of public administration has been reorganised. The emergence of European Union and single currency unit in Europe will bring drastic changes in the world trading system.

On the other hand, Western Asia has affected the structure of world economy due to the influx of oil money. African countries are the worst affected due to poverty and famines. Development evades them unfortunately.

Thus, innumerable variables and invariables are the determining factors of development and these factors deny specific principles to development. The variables and invariables depend upon domestic policies of government and international polices. Less developed countries find it difficult to manage internal resources while development programmes are implemented. They need capital, technology and technical know-how for accelerating economic growth. The domestic policies are conditioned in pursuit of market economy as liberalisation is a pre-requisite of financial assistance to meet balance of payments, deficit finance and investment gap. These nations need to create infrastructure for education, health, trade and industry. International cooperation in these areas provide opportunities for development and growth. Non-governmental organisations contribute effectively. Political stability is essential to carry out these programmes and implement development projects. Lack of political stability is the main constraint to third world countries as seen today in Rwanda and Somalia, etc. Newly decolonised nations are not free from domestic turmoils and pressure of power blocs. The nations that have recently achieved independence have inherited unresolved domestic and external problems which distract development activities. The worst problem is to identify these variables and invariables instantly. There is a chain of reactions. The newly independent nations are weak nations. Ultimately these nations continue to remain underdeveloped and deprived.

Under such conditions, it is all the more important to achieve development. In course of time several concepts of development have been evolved. Sustainable development is one of them. Sustainable development advocates the minimum acceptable principles to development, even though there are certain controversies and conflicts. It is again difficult to conclude that the limited principles advocated in the sustainable development concept would become universal.

NEED FOR INTERNATIONAL ENVIRONMENT MANAGEMENT

Each nation has to accept these realities and each nation has to pursue development simultaneously. Today each nation has understood that development and environment are inseparable and this fact denies any chance of ignorance.

The Stockholm Conference initiated the arguments for making development and environment achievable. In the process the efforts were made to identify areas in which the development and environment were increasingly contradictory to each other. Having understood the contradictions, the role of International Environmental Law was recognised for the first time formally while reviewing the performance of international environmental agreements and treaties. The Stockholm Conference has also recognised the need and necessity of international action, both to pursue and incorporate national attitudes towards environment and development so that acceptable and comprehensive global policies and law could be developed. At the same time, it is very relevant to mention here that the Conference has promoted certain basic understandings that need to be incorporated as policy changes towards environment and development. They are listed below:

(i) Environmental conditions are foundation of human development.

(ii) In each and every socio-political policy, the environment has to be integrated with.

(iii) International pursuits and national policies towards environment and development need to be integrated with national sovereignty. International institutions have to coordinate and cooperate with national and regional organisations and vice versa. In the promotion of environment and development, there will be new international actors and individual citizens even though these actors are not recognised in the International Law. This change has to be administered appropriately.

(iv) No nation can achieve environment and development in isolation. In other words, global dimension of environment impact and developmental dimensions cannot be pursued in isolation and ignored. Therefore, the environment, and development have to be one and the same.

(v) Technology transfer economic transfer and transfer of technical know-how are important aspects while the policies for environment and development are pursued.

In the last twenty years since the Stockholm Conference there has been a growth in international environmental agreements and treaties; there have been changes in global policies towards the environment and development which have successfully developed into a concept of sustainable development, there have been tremendous pressures on international institution, regional organisations and national institutions; there has been a tremendous demand for pollution free environment; there have been innumerable policy decisions towards safer environment and development and there have been successes and failures. The 1992 Earth Summit has given a comprehensive policy approaches towards international environment management. To achieve international environment management, different strategies have been successfully discussed and deliberated. The most important strategy is to develop international cooperation to accelerate sustainable development in the developing countries and in their domestic policies. To achieve this concept four policy dimensions have been proposed: (i) the international economy should provide a supportive climate for achieving environment and development goals and policies through trade liberalisation; (ii) making trade and environment mutually supportive; (iii) providing finance and technology to development and to overcome international debt; and (iv) encouraging micro economic policies conducive to environment and development. These policy objectives are successfully attempted to translate them into practice in the Uruguay Round of GATT Conference and recently established World Trade Organisation. There are various provisions incorporated in the Uruguay Round Agreements of GATT, 1994. In the recently concluded Singapore Summit on Labour Standards with reference to trade under WTO, there are different propositions and opinions among the participant countries. The recent Supreme Court judgement on employment of child labour in India is evident. Moreover the Supreme Court has given the order fixing the liability of the employer to Rs. 20,000 for the benefit of child labour. Its implementation is left to the administration of the States. In a recent interview on the Star News, it was revealed that the employment of child labour was still increasing in Delhi.

Therefore, there is a viable disproportionate gap between the policy and practice. To overcome this certain committed workforce and administrative machinery are inevitable. Recently the Supreme Court gave a deadline of one year till September 1997, to shift 192 factories situated near Taj Mahal in Agra. Similarly, in a judgement of November 1996 with reference to a Public Interest Litigation the Supreme Court ordered to close the factories situated in and around the capital, New Delhi, and shift them to places away from it. The workforce involved was expected to be 50000. The State Government has already initiated allotment of land for those factories that need to be shifted away. Further to add, in a later judgement of Supreme Court the owners of the factories are enjoined upon to make a compensation to workers if they do not shift the factories within the period stipulated and resort to close the factories without shifting. These judgements are placing sufficient challenges to the policies of development and environment. In shifting the industries, the capital investment for buildings and residential accomodation is massive. In a way, it is like opening a new factory.

Probably if the same amount is used for opening other factories it could provide employment to ten to twenty thousand workforce. India is one of the worst affected nations with regard to unemployment. Applying the provisions of environment to the trade practice will definitely cause concern and that improvement will bring a formidable challenge to the makers of socio-economic policies. For nations like Brazil forest is a primary source of income. On banning further deforestation, there may be economic collapse. Nigeria is having 80 per cent of its foreign trade through oil only. The oil industry is the most polluting industry. Whether to stop oil export or to starve, this is the biggest challenge when the environment is placed against trade practice. In Tamilnadu, child labour is predominantly used in match industry. Despite the various restrictions in the legislations and court orders, viable solutions are yet to be found. India is a country where the exploitation of child labour is a common phenomenon. The poor families earn their income and livelihood through the child labour.

Trade liberalisation is not totally practised in almost all the countries whether they are rich or poor. In fact, subsidy to agriculture is more in developed countries than in developing nations. Only the difference is that the subsidies in agriculture in developing nations are in the form of concession in fertilizer prices, etc. While we are studying the pattern of agriculture prices, the developing countries are the worst sufferers since they are the major importers. Due to subsidy in agriculture in developed countries the agicultural prices are inflated resulting in higher prices in the foreign trade. In the process, the beneficiaries are the rich nations and not the poor nations. Therefore, it is very difficult to suggest a comprehensive strategy to implement trade liberalisation. Further to add, transfer of technology is another important area where it is the common criticism that the obsolete technology is being transferred to Third World countries and these technologies are not environment friendly. Hence, there is another shortcoming of translating the strategy into practice globally. The growing international debt is almost a continuous phenomenon in the last two decades. Most of the Third World countries are the worst affected nations. It is practically not possible for either international institutions or rich countries to waive off the international debt since their economies equally depend upon funds that are to flow back. Therefore, there is another difficulty in combating this problem. But at the same time, development should not be at the cost of environment Since 1972, so many institutions have been conducting surveys on environment and development issues. GALLUP Institute has conducted a survey on the health of the Planet Earth and in its primary report, it is revealed that the developing nations are willing to achieve environmental protection in preference to development (USIA: 02334 (1992).

Therefore, it is equally difficult to conclude that development is the priority over environment even in the developing countries. Nevertheless this finding is not suggesting any solution. Poverty is the cause for under development which has to be eliminated. To eliminate it the development is the watchword.

The sovereignty of a nation is recognised in all the major deliberations in the UNO and the principle of sovereignty is also well recognised in International Law. International Court of Justice has enforced the principle of sovereignty of nations in all cases. Therefore, entering into environmental agreements may not solve the issues on environment as these are likely to interfere with every principle of sovereignty of nations. Particularly in the eyes of law unless there is a binding agreement among the member nations who have become parties to the environmental agreements and treaties, they cannot be compelled to implement the provisions of such International Environmental Agreements and Treaties. The predominant international environmental agreements are mainly protocols or conventions which do not have enforceability in the Court of Law under Conventional Law, International Law and Municipal Law. Under Indian Constitution, Article 50 incorporates treaties and agreements but not protocols and conventions. Similarly, in Britain where there is no written constitution unless there is valid agreement or treaty, the provision of such agreement or treaty cannot be enforced upon since the majority of the international environmental agreements or treaties are conventions or protocols. The European Community may bring enforcement of such conventions or protocols of international environmental agreements provided they are adopted within the jurisdiction of European Community Law so as to enforce among member nations. Under the US Constitution every International Agreement or Treaty has to be well recognised and adopted by the Legislature otherwise there is no sanctity before the Court of Law. Therefore, there is tremendous challenge for implementation of International Environmental Agreements and Treaties. To overcome this challenge, the sanction becomes infructuous. It is more important to achieve through international cooperation and understanding. There are certain principles of International Environmental Law which are not well recognised in the International Law. In view of it, the enforcement of the provisions of International Environmental Agreements cannot be presumed achieved.

While pursuing certain International Environmental Conventions and Protocols, the monitoring and enforcement powers are not generally granted to international institutions or to other member countries, taking into view the principles of sovereignty. According to UN Charter, by virtue of the consent of the nation after satisfying other considerations, the membership is granted. The consent of the member nation could be revoked at any point of time. Therefore, the power of sanction by the international institutions like UNO may be thwarted with revocation of its consent by the member nation.

There is another aspect, namely, North-South conflict in which South demands more development, and the development is to be sacrificed or postponed in order to achieve environment, as the North desires. The 1992 Rio Summit considered the demand of South and accordingly, the North nations agreed to share certain environmental costs and participate in the developmental projects of South nations. However, the question of sharing environmental costs has taken disproportionate form in many of the global discussions to the disadvantage of environment.

To fill the gap between the North and South is another dimension in respect of basic necessities. Therefore, it is not a simple task. At the same time, global environmental degradation cannot be allowed to continue since it will destroy the humanity as a whole irrespective of the South or North, irrespective of the cause of development or under development, legal sanctity or no sanctity and so on.

In view of above discussions, it is all the more important that international cooperation has to be evolved so as to promote the concept of sustainable development through International Environmental Law with the active participation of international institutions and for the same, the International Environment Management is most essential today.

CHAPTER 2

Conflicts and Controversies: Sustainable Development

The concept of sustainable development has evolved in the last two decades even though the most acceptable definition is given in the Brundtland Report, 1987, and this defination is confirmed in the Rio Earth Summit, 1992. This is more evident in the recently held 'Global Warming' conference in July 1996 in Geneva.

It has grown beyond the narrow national interests and nationalism. It has added a new dimension to globalism. The sustainable development demands the greatest urgency and international cooperation in all forms including political process, economic values and legal enforcement through international environmental law.

The Commission on Sustainable Development was established in 1993 for monitoring and coordinating the implementation of principles of sustainable development even though there are conflicts and controversies.

Evolution of Sustainable Development

The Brundtland Report, 1987, is the key statement of sustainable development, (Kirby 1995). The Brundtland Report also known as 'Our Common Future', was submitted in August, 1987, by an independent special commission consisting of government officials, economists and scientists. It later adopted the name of World Commission on Environment and Development. This commission was chaired by the

Norwegian Prime Minister, Mrs. Gro Harlien Brundtland, in pursuant of UN General Assembly resolution 38/161 adopted at the 38th Session of 1983 (WCED 1987).

Definitions

There are innumerable definitions on sustainable development and some of them are discussed here. Sustainable development is the development which is 'likely to achieve lasting satisfaction of human needs and improvement of the quality of human life' (Allen 1980).

The sustainable development as applied to the Third World is the increasing of material standard of living of the poor at the 'grassroots' level and its primary objective in general is 'reducing the absolute poverty of the world's poor through providing lasting and secure livelihoods that minimise resource depletion, environmental degradation, cultural disruption and social instability' (Barbier 1987).

· 'Sustainable development aims for promoting growth, alleviating poverty, and protecting the environment that are mutually supportive objectives in the long run but not in the short run' (World Bank 1987). The Brundtland Report, 1987, defines sustainable development as 'development meeting the needs of the present without compromising the ability for future generations to meet their own needs' (WCED 1987).

The Brundtland Report: Popularity

The Brundtland Report's definition of sustainable development is widely accepted due to many reasons. First international institutions like World Bank, GATT/WTO, FAO, WMO, UNESCO and other organisations of UN systems have accepted this definition when the policy decisions are made and implemented. Secondly, the members of UNO have accepted and adopted WCED report vide resolution 42/187, on 11 December, 1987. Thirdly, the UNEP governing council has accepted the WCED report as a guideline for further UNEP action on 19 June, 1987. Fourthly, all the nations including super powers have accepted it since it is prepared by an independent body of scientists, economists and politicians. Fifthly, it survives 'because it appears to build bridges between the demand of environmentalists and developers' (Kirby 1996). Sixthly, David W. Pearce states that 'it is an article of faith' like justice, equality and freedom (Ibid).

Origin of Sustainable Development

Many authors refer to the World Conservation Strategy, 1980, which is the origin of concept of sustainable development (John Kirby 1996), (Michael 1987), and (Adams W.M. 1990). It is also traced back to the documents of South Pacific Commission 1980 (Adams W. M. 1990). Adams has conclusively argued that the origin of the concept of sustainable development may be traced back to the 1960s and 1970s after examining it under five themes viz (1) preservation and conservation in tropical countries, (2) the rise of tropical ecological science in Africa, (3) the growing global reach of scientific concern particularly of man and biosphere programmes, (4) the rise of perceptions of global environmental crisis, and lastly, the 1972 Stockholm Conference (Ibid).

The above analysist of Adams shows the emergence of the concept of sustainable development from national to regional and finally to global. Under the UNO system the emergence of the concept of sustainable development may be traced back to the proposal of Sweden to Economic and Social Council to convene International Conference on Human Environment, on 29 May, 1968, and the resolution was passed in the Council on 30 July, 1968, recommending for the same to UN General Assembly for its approval.

The UN General Assembly decided on 3 December, 1968, to convene the United Nations Conference on Human Environment in 1972 vide its resolution 2398 (XXIII). This is not only the beginning of the concept of sustainable development but also the beginning of institutional framework towards sustainable development.

Linking Environment and Development

On 3 December, 1968, UN General Assembly desired a report by the Secretary General of the Economic and Social Council to be submitted in 1969, and report was submitted accordingly. The report reads that the environmental problems are global affecting both developed and developing countries and that environmental policies must be as part of the long term development of resources for economic and social purposes.

The 1972 Stockholm Conference on Human Environment confirmed these aspects of linking environment and development and the endorsement is found in the 26 principles adopted at the conference on 16 June, 1972. Linking environment and development has given birth to the ideology of sustainable development in the Brundtland Report, 1987, and the recommendations of the Second (Economic and Financial) Committee on Environmental Perspectives to the year 2000 and beyond. General Assembly adopted these recommendations and the Report vide its resolutions 42/186 and 42/187. The recommendations of the 'Environmental Perspective to the year 2000 and beyond' include multifaceted dimensions of environment and development and the means and methods for achievement.

The Brundtland Report has gone ahead of linking environment and development to sustainable development which discussed the issues of environment and development not only for the present but also for the future generations. This concept of sustainable development is endorsed in the Declaration of 27 principles and Agenda 21 of the Earth Summit 1992.

Concept: Policy and Strategy

The Brundtland Report finds two-way relationship between

development and environment. First, the economic development leads to environmental damage and secondly, the environmental damage affects future productivity. Mrs. Gro Harlem Brundtland, in her keynote speech at the 6th EADI General Conference in Oslo, 27 June, 1990, after three years of the WCED Report, has reiterated that the economy and ecology are becoming increasingly interwoven in a seamless web of cause and effect. The environmental problems that countries face depend upon the stage of development.

There are three patterns of environmental problems depending upon the stage of development. First, some environmental problems decline as income increases, e.g. health and sanitation. Secondly, some environmental problems worsen initially but subsequently improve as income increases, e.g. air and water pollution. Thirdly, there are certain indicators of environmental stress that worsen the emissions of carbon, and of nitrogen oxides and municipal wastes as income increases (WDR1992).

In 'The Limits to Growth' it is mentioned that if the present resource exploitation, food production and industrialisation continue unchanged, the limits to growth will be reached in the next 100 years (Meadows 1972). Therefore no growth is suggested. Moreover many essential resources and generations of many pollutants have exceeded the sustainable limits which may reduce the per capita output, energy use and industrial production (Meadows 1992).

After 20 years since the publication of "The Limits to Growth' the book 'Beyond the Limits' is published by the same authors and they have reiterated that having reached the limits to the sources of materials and energy that sustain growth, and having reached the limits to the sinks that absorb the waste products of growth, the signals like erosion of ozone layer, global warming, desertification, climatic change, acid rain and loss of biodiversity are growing. The remedy lies in the slow down of growth and ultimately the growth is stopped (Ibid).

No growth means no development; no development means

the South and North gap; and the poverty, malnutrition, unsafe water, insanitation, high infant mortality and uneven development persist. Therefore, the concept of sustainable development needs more clarity to remove this conflict and controversy.

Developing countries view global environmental issues from a historical perspective. It is argued that most of the environmental damage originates from the industrialised nations and the no growth concept should be applied to them. Therefore, the priorities of economic activities of developed nations have to be altered.

The developed countries view the global environmental problems on the population growth, low agricultural production and the exploitation of natural resources of the developing nations and feel that the developing countries are to change their policies. In fact, population growth is not the main source of environmental degradation, as the maximum emissions of carbon dioxide and greenhouse gases are from the five per cent population representing developed nations. The South is having more forests, and more natural resources with less emission of carbon dioxide and greenhouse gases. The maximum energy consumption is in the North. Therefore these arguments and counter arguments are complicating the realisation of sustainable development (Chichilinisky 1996).

Environmental measures must anticipate, prevent and attack the causes of environmental degradation. The important measures are environmental taxes on environmentally campaign activities and products, the reduction or elimination of subsidies wherever they encourage activities which are environmentally harmful, and emission charges or fees, tradeable permits including tax incentives. The international organisations like World Bank, IMF and other financial institutions, and GATT/WTO are insisting on these measures when policy decisions are finalised on developmental loans, grants and aid in the trade. In practice, the political considerations and the principles of populism supervenes these economic measures. Under such conditions the concept of sustainable development is found in conflict and controversy.

Lack of effective sustainable development indicators will create more conflicts and controversies between developed and developing countries while monitoring and coordinating the realisation of sustainable development.

Needs

The concept of needs introduces the question of redistribution of resource as to satisfy the human needs and aspirations of an expanding developing world population as it is the central theme of sustainable development (WCED 1987). However, the 'basic needs' is a relative term as in the industrialised countries once what were regarded as luxuries, are now regarded as necessities.

In the distribution of income 30 years ago, the 20 per cent increased their share from 70 per cent to 85 per cent (*The Economic* 1996). Thus on a world scale, the prospect of maintaining the standared of the rich while improving the condition of the poor is impossible under present economic systems. World poverty remains the main cause and effect of environmental degradation. Those who are poor will continue to destroy their immediate environment in order to survive. In fact, the gap is widening between rich and poor. During the period of 1980-91, GNP per capita increased by an average of 1 per cent in the South, and in sub-Sahara it has declined by 1.2 per cent. It has increased by 2.3 per cent in the North (Robin1996). The growth of population is uneven among rich and poor nations. It is estimated that population in developing countries is projected to increase from 68.5 per cent to 79.9 per cent in 2000 AD. The continuing increase in population in the South demands more basic needs unlike in the case of the rich. (Common 1995).

To meet these needs more production is essential but this may result in environmental crises. Similarly lack of basic needs like housing and health will also add to environmental crisis (WCED 1987). The development includes economic growth and human development. More needs means more environmental crisis which will be a challenge to sustainable development.

Future Generations

The third aspect of sustainable development is that it should be achieved 'without compromising the ability of future generations to meet their own needs'. This is proposed on the basis of principle of equity.

As Solow states there is only moral obligation on the present generation to sacrifice the comforts of present in favour of future generations. It is purely a principle of equity and moreover nothing is found evident that the future generations will realise the sacrifice which is also expected from the them too to preserve the natural resource for the future generations. It is also not sure that the future generations may have the same technology and economic system for which it is essential or otherwise. However, he agrees, 'we free-ride on each other and we free-ride on the future' (Solow 1991). The concept of future generations is viewed differently too. Future generations must not be subjected to unacceptable risks of death owing to environment or to the catastrophes caused by the present.

The present and future generations may have to sacrifice some of their freedoms in the process of preserving for future generations (Tonn 1988). The economists have developed certain means and methods to achieve this in the management of natural resources.

The first is the 'cake-eating' principle. According to it, the finite resources are to be exploited within the accepted time framework. To avoid the depletion of natural resources, the recycling and susbstituting are suggested even though these will not stop the depletion of resources ultimately.

Discounting is a second concept devised by economists and employed by governments and business and it saves future liabilities in terms of present costs. Discounting assumes that money can be invested now and accumulate interest. Consequently, a discount rate can be applied which ensures at least that money invested now will yield sufficient return to deny future liabilities. This is known as 'Hotelling Rule'.

The third concept is the Hartwick Rule. According to this rule, by maintaining 'Keep Capital Intact', the man-made capital will be increased to substitute wherever it is possible to maintain constant 'Total Capital Stock'.

In the absence of proper property rights natural resources are bound to be overused due to the problem of open access. This is known as the 'Tragedy of the Commons' according to H. G. Hardwin Michael Common, and many others deny that the tragedy of the commons do not apply to natural resources as the problem arises not in the context of common property, but in the context of not clearly defined property rights (Commons 1995) and (Turner 1994). Natural resources are overused leading to depletion and extinct when property rights are absent (Chichilinisky 1996). The international co-operation and participation by member nations will ensure the proper conservation and preservation of natural resources so that the problems of open access which may result in inefficient use of natural resources could be solved according to Scaffer Model. Lack of incentive for cooperation may not resort to the free-rider instinct to detect as Olson argues in his 'Logic of Collective Action'. The problem of Prisioners' Dilemma causes a serious concern to the management of natural resources. Therefore a system has to be devised to overcome these problems in order to achieve sustainable development.

Needs to Reconcile

The environment meets three basic needs of man: the sources of natural resources for production; natural goods—landscape, sceneries and views, wilderness, all aspects of wildlife, which are valued in contributing to the quality of life; and the atmosphere, land and oceans as repositories for its waste products (Lenihan 1979). The environment performs four functions: capital stock; waste sink; amenity base; and life supportive systems (Common 1995).

Capital stock consists of non-renewable and renewable resources. A renewable resource regenerates itself like fish and trees. A non-renewable resource is fixed in overall quantity since there is no natural reproduction except on geological time scales. The waste sink relates to the assimilative capacity and the pollution results where the residual flow exceeds assimilative capacity. The amenity services flow from the environment to individuals with recreational facilities, pleasure and stimulation. The fourth function is the life supportive system. Biosphere, air, solar radiation and bio-diversity are some of the elements of life supportive system.

Today it is found that UVB radiation affects living things and it causes skin cancer. This is due to loss of assimilative capacity of ozone layer in the stratosphere. The loss of biodiversity and the change in atmospheric concentration of greenhouse gases are found increasing in the last 50 years (Chichilinisky 1996). Global warming is related to manufacturing. Green house gas effect is directly related to population growth and deforestation. Climate change is related to biosphere in total. Therefore strategies are needed to save the life supportive system, resource base, amenity base and waste sink.

The world conservation strategy was prepared in 1980 with three objectives. First it is related to the maintenance of crop land, control the discharge of pollutants and maintenance of coastal wetlands. The second objective is 'genetic diversity' to prevent extinction. The third objective is aiming for 'sustainable utilisation' of natural resources, live stocks and plant including their preservation (Adams 1990). The 'Limits to Growth' and 'Beyond the Limits' advocate no growth model even though the pessimism of limits to growth is presented in a modified version in the 'Beyond the Limits' (Meadows 1972 and 1992). The anti-growth model of conservation of nature is reflected and it is argued that economic growth is inevitable to eradicate poverty and improve standard of living of more than one-third of world population. There are three arguments. First, the environment is essential for the well being of all persons and not excluding people who starve and suffer from poverty. Secondly, the causes of environmental degradation are due to mismanagement of natural resources and not otherwise. Thirdly, solving environmental degradation may involve correcting economic distortions and providing incentives for resource conservation and resource reduction (Pearce 1993).

To reconcile this problem, the Stockholm Conference has linked environment and development and it has established UNEP to monitor and co-ordinate the 109 recommendations and 26 principles adopted in this regard.

The Brundtland Report 1987 has suggested sustainable development as an improvement to linking environment and development so as to ensure meeting the needs and aspirations of present and future generations. In 1992, Earth Summit confirmed it. WCED has demanded a need for change in national and international policies to achieve sustainable development for the following reasons: first, the environmental stresses and patterns of economic development are linked to one another as energy and agricultural policies cause deforestation and greenhouse effect. Secondly, environmental and economic problems are linked to many social and political factors like population growth, poverty and cultural values. Finally, it is not restricted to one nation alone but it has transboundaries (WCED 1987).

All nations are not uniformly contributing to environmental problems of global warming, greenhouse effect, ozone depletion and the disposal of waste. It demands two approaches to solve. First approach may deal with the environmental policies outside the institutional framework of international organisations and the second is within the institutional framework of international organisations. There are many environmental policies in the first approach and some of them are mentioned here. These include regulating mechanism and incentives. First, the policy instrument is to pursue the people to cooperate with environmental policy. Secondly, it is through direct controls that include regulations limiting the permissible levels of emissions and mandatory processes or equipment. Thirdly, it is through regulation of economy. These are taxation, levying duties, penalties and fines, licensing and subsidies. Finally, it is through investment in research and education, and preventing mechanism of systems and equipments (William 1979).

In additions to these, the developed nations may extend financial aid, technical know-how, transfer of technology and concessional loans and grants to developing countries so that there is equal participation in reducing environmental degradation (WDR 1992).

The second approach is within the institutional framework of international organisations such as the UN and its organisations, World Bank, IMF, WTO, non-governmental organisations and regional bodies.

For better coordination and cooperation of these two approaches, there is a need for devising a system which will be impartial, consistent and acceptable to all and it is possible through international environmental agreements which have given birth to international environmental law.

These are two approaches that are aiming to remove conflicts and controversies while the concept of sustainable development is achieved.

Chapter 3

Problems of Compliance

Having looked at the general principles we now turn to the question of agreements that are devised, agreed and implemented. The major problem is the one of securing compliance, and we begin by outlining a framework within which to analyse this. The compliance is inclusive of implementation and enforcement of international environmental agreements.

TWO SCHOOLS

There are two schools of thought on the aspects of compliance. There are three aspects belonging to one school of thought where the compliance depends upon the voluntary co-operation among the member nations. According to the second school of thought the compliance is secured by virtue of the obligations accepted in the international agreements. The first aspect of the former school of thought says that the self-interest of the participating members of international environmental agreements is the deciding force behind the compliance. The second aspect reveals the moral responsibility towards the welfare of the humanity which will be the force behind the compliance. The third aspect states the fear of isolation by the other nations when a nation refuses compliance.

Voluntary Cooperation

Voluntary cooperation among nations may secure compliance of international environmental agreements. Every nation may realise the environmental degradation is undesirable and harmful to the humanity. As living and non-living things are depleted at an alarming rate and life support systems such as air and water that have become increasingly polluted, it has become necessary to organise the human activities to remove these threats. Global warming occurs when the earth's atmosphere partially traps more and more gases—mainly carbon dioxide from burning fossil fuels, but also methane (natural gases), nitrous oxide,, chlorofluora carbons (CFC), and other gases. These gases cause the atmosphere to reflect heat back to the earth's surface rather than allowing to escape. Contribution of each greenhouse gas to global warming 1980-1990 is given below:

24%	CFC	:	Chlorofluoro Carbon
6%	N_2O	:	Nitrous Oxide
15%	CH_4	:	Methane
55%	CO_2	:	Carbon Dioxide

The 1991 report of the Inter-governmental Panel on Climate Change predicts that without concerted international action to control emissions, average global temperatures are likely to rise by about 1 degree Celsius by 2025, or by 3 degrees Celsius before 2100. The expected contribution of human activities to global warming from 1980-1990 would be: energy 46% agriculture 9%; forestry 18%; industry (CFC) 24%; and others 3%.

Measures

There are many measures that can reduce carbon-dioxide emissions to limit global warming. These measures include:

- reducing fossil-fuel use through increases in energy efficiency;
- shifting towards natural gas (for the same energy out-put, natural gas produces only 57% of the amount of carbon dioxide produced by coal);

- replacing fossil fuel use with alternative energy technologies; and
- eliminating forest loss by better management of forests and large scale reforestation (forests absorb carbon dioxide).

Acid rain is the result of the chemical transformation of sulpher dioxide and nitrogen oxides in the atmosphere. These pollutants are released by the most important sources such as electricity generating plants, mineral smelters, industrial installations, motor vehicles, and residential and commercial establishments using fuels.

Technologies

A few technologies available to reduce acid rain are given below:

- producing of fuels low in sulphur and nitrogen content;
- using combustion modification technologies and post-combustion emission controls which allow removal of 50 to 90 per cent of the sulphur dioxide in coal fired electric power plants;
- using the catalytic converter to reduce emissions of nitrogen oxides in new cars burning unleaded petrol;
- increasing fuel efficiency; and
- sharing vehicles and limiting private car use.

Implementation

The implementation of these measures will reduce the environmental degradation. This is possible through concerted negotiation and international cooperation. According to the first school of thought the voluntary cooperation is source of compliance of international environmental agreements. The success of voluntary cooperation is measured in terms of participation to the compliance of international environmental agreements.

Mechanisms

The mechanisms to ensure compliance with these agreements are specifically enumerated in the agreements. Each agreement stipulates mechanisms for securing compliance with the agreement. It may be found in three stages. First stage deals with the confirmation of participation to agreements by the parties. In each agreement there is a specific provision on notification of the agreement and confirmation of participation to agreement. Second stage refers to the jurisdiction and enumeration of obligations agreed to by the parties to the agreement. These provisions help the member states to plan and make strategies for securing compliance with the agreement. Third stage deals with the details of enforcement mechanism of the agreement. It is also known as the provisions for sanction for compliance against non-compliance.

FIRST STAGE OF COMPLIANCE

Ratification

The first stage of the compliance is associated with the ratification of the agreement. Ratification of a treaty is an act of confirmation of participation to agreements. Issuing notification of the agreement is the beginning to proceed towards ratification. Confirmation of participation succeeds the notification. As soon as the ratification of a treaty is performed the member state carries out certain measures. These measures may be broadly divided into three and are briefly discussed here.

1. It brings suitable legislative measures for incorporating the obligations of the agreement for enforceability in the municipal law. It may be brought into through amendments to the Constitution, introducing new legislation, or administrative orders, etc.
2. The member state may authorise the existing administrative machinery or it may establish a new

machinery for securing compliance of the obligations stipulated and agreed to in the agreement.
3. The financial arrangements are made to ensure the compliance with the agreement treaty.

Ratification is essential for bringing the agreement/treaty into force. Ratification is also a prerequisite for ensuring the compliance of agreement. Many international environmental agreements are yet to come into force for want of ratification.

Requisite Members

There is no standard practice to decide the minimum number of states to ratify the agreement. Twenty states are required to ratify the 1989 Basel Convention on the Control of Transboundary Movement of Hazardous Wastes. In the case of United Nations Convention on the Laws of the Sea, sixty states are needed to ratify the agreement even though the 157 states have attended and signed the Convention in 1982. All the 34 states who are the signatories of the Convention on Long Range Transboundary Air Pollution are required to ratify the agreement. Therefore the requisite number (of states) varies from agreement to agreement that is essential for ratification so as to bring it into force.

Voluntary Cooperation

The ratification is purely an act of voluntary cooperation. Under the Charter of United Nations no nation may be compelled to become member of any agreement or association including the UNO. Similarly no nation can be compelled to ratify the agreement. It is also equally true that no nation may be compelled to sign the treaties as one of the signatories leave apart the ratification. India and China initially had declined to sign the Montreal Convention even though subsequently they became its members in 1995.

In Estonia, new legislation is being prepared aimed to

implement the provisions of the convention. The bill will then be presented to the parliament for approval before effecting its ratification. In the United Kingdom no legislative action is required for ratification of the convention or the agreement. In India the legislative action is essential for ratification.

SECOND STAGE

The second stage of the compliance is associated with the implementation of the agreement/treaty. Legislative or administrative action may be essential for implementation. In the United Kingdom administrative action is sufficient. The legislative action helps the provisions of the agreement enforceable in the municipal law. If the party in power fails to pass the legislation for want of majority in the parliament the ratification is not possible. Despite ratification of the agreement, the state may not be able to provide infrastructure to implement the obligations due to weak administrative system or lack of finance. These problems are common to Third World countries.

The implementation may be delayed or there may be a deviation in the agreed obligations in the convention. This problem is seen in many international environmental agreements. The Treaty Banning Nuclear Weapons Tests in the Atmosphere in Outer Space and Underwater was signed in 1963 and it came into force the same year. The U.S.A., France, and former USSR oppose a complete ban on all forms of testing even though, on account of this treaty, radiation threat from atmosphere contamination has declined substantially since the 1963 ban. Due to opposition from the U.S.A., the permanent protection is modified into 50-year moratorium in the Protocol on Environment Protection 1991. Convention on Wet lands of international importance especially as Waterfall Habitat (RAMSAR) 1971 came into existence in 1975, and due to lack of commitment by developed nations to provide financial and technical assistance to developing countries, the level of funding promised has not been forthcoming. In 1982, numerous amendments were made to the International Convention for the Regulation of Whaling 1946.

One of the amendments was to phase out Commercial Whaling over the years. The ban became effective in 1986. Now Iceland, Norway and Japan are seeking IWC sanction to resume commercial whaling. Despite the 1985 Vienna Convention for the Protection of the Ozone Layer and the 1987 Montreal Protocol on substances that deplete the ozone layer, there is continuing depletion of the earth's stratosphere ozone layer by reactive chlorine and bromine from man-made CFC, halons, and related substances.

In spite of having concluded and committed to the obligations enunciated in the various aspects of Global Commons in more than 140 agreements, the global environmental degradation continues to cause concern.

ANALYSIS

The above mentioned problems of compliance can be analysed briefly in the subsequent chapters. Some of the important problems of compliance with these agreements are mentioned here.

- Transboundary environmental problems like climatic change, the preservation of diversity, protection of the oceans, decisions about how best to manage shared resources like Antarctica, or the difficult task of promoting sustainable development go well beyond anything one country or even a group of countries can accomplish on its own.
- Representation and voting procedures do not guarantee that all countries and interests are treated fairly.
- Scientific and political considerations are not balanced in ways that ensure that the wisest possible policies will emerge.

- Linkages among environmental concerned and the policy issues are rarely explored or crafted adequately.
- Effective monitoring and enforcement arrangements are not implemented.
- The treaty making process is constrained by the global interplay of domestic policies. In the final analysis only agreements that are politically acceptable to national leaders will be approved.
- If too few countries ratify an agreement, the cumulative efforts of those living upto their promises may be insufficient to reverse the problem.
- Most global environmental agreements worked out through ad-hoc negotiations include weak monitoring and enforcement provisions.
- Very few nations participate in the negotiations even though the global environmental problems are universal.

FREE RIDER PROBLEMS

These problems have resulted into lack of participation to international environmental agreements. This is considered to be a "free-rider problem". The free-rider problem will be examined with the help of some theories in the subsequent chapters.

Provision of Enforcement

After examining various aspects of the free-rider problem one of the suggestions is the provision for enforcement through an external force. The external force may bring complete participation to the international environmental agreements. This is pertaining to the second school of thought that enforcement is essential for extensive cooperation among the nations leading to effective compliance. Each agreement has specific provisions for enforcement of the compliance of the obligations agreed to by the member-nations of the agreements.

Weak Law

The international environmental law is weak; it lacks enforceability; it is a soft law; and it is subject to the consent of the nations on whom the provisions are applicable. In the monitoring system it is generally said that the dispute among the parties may be solved by negotiation and these nations may decide the process of settlement. The third party interference is excluded for the settlement of any disputes.

Consent

The reference of the dispute to the International Court of Justice is subject to the consent of all the parties to the disputes. If there is no consent given there is no application of them against the nation. The sovereignty of the nation is another stumbling block. The U.N.O. has recognized it. The Third World countries expressed their reservations in the participation of the negotiations. According to them the development precedes environment. The developing countries have to depend upon the natural resources for their survival unlike industrial countries.

Change of Priority

The technology available to them is obsolete and not friendly to the environment. The poor countries do not have money to invest on environmental activities; they do not have the infrastructures facilities to have proper research and development. The developed countries look for raw materials available from the least developed countries. The developing countries depend upon the natural resources for exports to meet imports. To provide basic amenities of health, education and other welfare measures including the programmes for eradication of poverty and other welfare measures is on top priority rather than the environment protection. Under such circumstances they prefer development to environment resulting into non-participation to international environmental agreements. This is discussed in the subsequent chapters.

In conclusion, the suggestion is made, in the last chapter, for achieving effective participation to international agreements so that there is sustainable development and it is known as "Empowerment of Sustainable Development".

CHAPTER 4

General Features of International Environmental Law

International environmental law has emerged as one of the means to achieve sustainable development through international cooperation for implementing environmental agreements. It acts as an effective link between municipal law and international law while addressing the global problems of environmental degradation and management of commons towards development. Justice Nagendra Singh, the then President of International Court of Justice, had identified the following three important roles of international environmental law to achieve sustainable development:

1. to strengthen and extend the application of existing laws and international agreements in support of sustainable development;
2. to recognise and respect the reciprocal rights and responsibilities of individuals and states regarding sustainable development, and to apply new norms for state and interstate behaviour to enable this to be achieved; and
3. to reinforce existing methods and develop new procedures for avoiding and resolving disputes on environmental and resource management issues (*Legal Principles and Recommendations,* WCED, 1987).

The growth, general features, and principles of international environmental law will be briefly discussed here. The growth and development will explain the slow and steady emergence of international environmental law. The general features of international environmental law will address its basic sources. The principles of international environmental law will give a brief introduction of the basic elements with which the court of law interprets and enforces the international environmental agreements.

Growth

International environmental law has rapidly grown since the 1972 Stockholm Conference. Six of the 26 principles adopted in the conference are stressing the need for international cooperation in accordance with UN Charter and the principles of international law as envisaged in the principle 21. Prof. Gerd Winter maintains that environmental law is regulating the relationship between man and nature. He narrates this relationship in four phases which describe the growth of international environmental law. The first of the relationship is known as the **circular economy** or **cyclical economy** in which there is no specific environmental protection law since the legal norms regarding the cooperative life of human beings also provide for the preservation of natural resources. This is the phase of common property management regime in which social norms regulate property rights. The second phase is the prevention of **exploitation of nature by man** in which the laws aim for efficient allocation of natural resources and preventing environmental damage by means of police power. This is also the phase of disintegration of common property management regime. The third phase is known as **the planned management of nature.** During this phase the environmental allocation law has become the environmental protection law. This started in 1970s. There are three characteristic features of environmental protection law such as defining the 'tolerance thresholds' between nature and human activities, identifying 'technically feasible' to avoid damage, and developing the concept of 'interventionistic orientation' in which the laws propose prohibitions, commands, permit provisos, taxes, and subsidies. The fourth phase of the growth of international environmental law is **'thinking about new solutions'.** In this phase, the 'procedural solutions' are proposed and are put underway. This is the phase of 'tolerance limits' of nature and 'soft technology' leading to a 'new qualitative orientation of environmental law'. The 'cooperation principle' is the theme of this phase to solve the problem of 'non-enforcement' of international environmental law (Winter 1989). The disintegration of common property management regime has led to severe environmental degradation in course of time since 19th century. Incidentally this period happened to be the beginning of the fast economic development. This is the period that laid foundation of scientific advancement and discoveries, economic development, a change in war strategy, and World Wars in the 20th century. With this background one would argue that the fifth phase may be the 'empowerment of sustainable development' in the 21st century in the growth of international environmental law.

General Features

The sources of international environmental law consist of various principles that are purely reflecting the concept of sustainable development, and all the general principles of international law are equally applicable. However the general principles concerning natural resources and environmental interferences recommended by the WCED legal experts group, Articles 1-8, have in common that they are applicable to all instances of the use of natural resource or of an environmental interference in any part of the world. Even though the recommendations of the legal expert group of WCED have been adopted by the General Assembly they do not form the basic source of international environmental law.

Let us discuss certain important sources of international environmental law.

The first important source of international environmental law is the **'conventional norms'.** Many treaties fall in this category. The most important characteristic features of the conventional norms that are found in the treaties are: the importance of implementing measures being taken by the contracting parties; supervisory mechanisms to review implementation; procedures to ease the process of modifying the treaties; action plans for further measures; and mechanisms of cooperation, either by the creation of new institutions or the utilisation of existing mechanisms. Measures for implementation are of two kinds such as self-executing and non self-executing. The self-executing provisions may be spelt out clearly or if they are found implicitly or implied then they are known as non self-executing provisions. In the self-executing provisions no additional initiative is required to implement the provisions and in the non self-executing provisions additional actions are needed to implement them. With reference to supervising implementation generally the states parties to treaties supervise implementation by other states parties as the treaties are made in good faith. Sometimes they may propose for third party supervision. The third parties for this purpose are jointly agreed upon. Normally the international organisations may perform this function. There may be simplified procedures for bringing suitable amendments to the treaties wherever necessary. This is an important norm. With reference to action plans and programmes, the precise obligations are created among states parties to undertake or refrain from specific conduct. The nature of environmental problems make it more difficult to define and specify the obligations. Therefore one has to depend upon the established principles that are legally binding manifesting the will of states to accept obligations. As such there is a need for permanent organs of cooperation among states to environmental agreements.

The second important source is **the customary international law.** The customary international law has emerged from different stages in its evolution. The formulation of non-binding principles, the repetition of specific rules, the principle of consensus are some of the features of customary international law. These norms are codified in state practice. Newly emerged customary rules of international law are like that no state will cause or allow its territory to be used to cause damage to the environment of other states, and the duty to co-operate. These rules are incorporated in principles 21 and 24 of Stockholm Declaration.

The third source is **the general principles of law** recognised by civilised nations. The general principles of law that are common to the major legal systems of the world are identified in this category. Recently emerging rules include the principle of preventing damage to environment, the principle that reparations should be made for environmental damage, and the principle that the survival of endangered species should be assured.

The fourth principle is **the judicial decisions and teachings** of the most highly qualified publicists of the various nations.

The fifth source is **the new sources of law** such as binding resolutions and non-binding texts, and if there is any violation in its obligations a complaint can be filed with the Security Council. The non-binding resolutions are directives, recommendations, programmes of action, and declaration of principles.

Principles

There are certain principles that have become the basis for interpretation and enforcement of international environmental law.

The first principle is **the preventive principle.** This principle emerged at the earliest stage in the development of European environmental policy. The preventive principle can be traced back to international environmental treaties and other international acts since 1930s. It is based on the premise that prevention is better than cure. Each country follows its own means and measures to prevent environmental damage. In the 1972 Stockholm Conference, the Environment Impact Assessment directive has been formulated at international level to monitor and coordinate. In many of the state nations town planning is to play an important role.

The next principle is **the precautionary principle.** The precautionary principle can be traced back to mid-1980s. This principle has been in domestic application, much earlier to this period, in the then West Germany. This principle provides guidance in the development and application of international environmental law where there are scientific uncertainties. The Ministerial Declaration of the Second Sea Conference 1987 has recognised it. The 1990 Bergen Ministerial Declaration on Sustainable Development in the ECE Region recognises that in order to achieve sustainable development, policies must be based on the precautionary principle. There are basically two characteristic features: the lack of scientific evidence cannot form an excuse for environmental degradation and the environmental policies need to be based on the notions anticipating, preventing, and attacking the causes of environmental degradation. It has now received international recognition particularly in the protection of the marine environment and the instruments adopted at UNCED 1992.

The third principle is **the subsidiary principle.** Subsidiary is the principle which is carried out at lower level of the formation. In other words the subsidiary principle is generally invoked where a case is made for decisions at the lowest level of the organisation or establishment. The roots of the subsidiary principle may be found in three sources. First source is the catholic s ocial philosophy. The second source is the political and constitutional theory. The third source is the argument of efficiency of decision making at decentralisation. The most important source is the constitutional system. In constitutional system the powers are distributed in three ways such as enumerated powers, implied powers, and the principle of proportionality. In environmental issues the principle of proportionality is adopted (Dommen (Ed.) 1993).

The fourth principle is **the polluter pays principle.** The polluter pays principle envisages that the costs of pollution should be borne by the person responsible for causing the pollution and consequential costs. The application of this principle depends upon the interpretations, particular cases and situations. This principle has brought more controversial discussions in the Rio Earth Summit 1992. The South has demanded more financial assistance from the North in combating the environmental degradation in the South. There are practical implications on the allocation of economic obligations in relation to environmentally damaging activities, particularly in relation to liability, the use of economic instruments, and the application of rules relating to competition and subsidy.

The fifth principle is **the user pays principle** even though it is also considered as a part of the polluter pays principle. This principle emanated from the OECD in 1988. According to this principle all resource users should pay for the full long run marginal social cost of the use of a resource and related services, including any associated treatment costs. The user pays principle is applied when resources are being used and consumed and when they are discharged.

The sixth is **the principle of common but differentiated responsibility.** This has developed from the application of equity in general international law. This principle has taken into account the special needs of developing countries for their development, in the application and interpretation of the international environmental law. This principle is incorporated in the 7th Principle of the Rio Declaration 1992. This principle has two elements. The first concerns the common responsibility of states for the protection of the environment at the national, regional and global levels. The second element concerns the need to take into account its contribution and ability to prevent, reduce and control the environmental degradation and its related problems.

The seventh principle is **the principle of intergenerational equity** which is accepted in the Rio Earth Summit 1992. According to this principle, environmental policies should aim to provide sufficient scope for preserving the nature for future generations.

Chapter 5

International Environmental Agreements

A treaty is an agreement in which all the details have presumably been worked out and expressed in the document to which each signing party agrees. A convention is an agreement in which parties agree on a general framework that is expected to be supplemented in the future by one or more protocols that work out the details. The international environmental agreements fall under either of the categories. In addition to them there are also declarations which are equally included in the international environmental agreements. The earliest international environmental agreement known is the European Treaty on the Conservation of Birds Useful to Agriculture,1902, even though the history of international agreements on natural resources goes back many centuries, to the time when countries sought to agree on navigation rules to cover ocean passages. The growth of such treaties has been rapid in the 20th century due to environmental problems involving many countries. In 1972 Stockholm Conference, the international environmental law was recognised as one of the means to achieve better cooperation among the nations to find solutions to the environmental problems. The Brundtland Report has codified principles of international environmental law based upon the international environmental agreements so as to achieve the Sustainable Development. In this chapter, the nature, the kinds and the parties to international environmental agreements will be briefly discussed.

Nature

There are two types of international environmental agreements and they are known as bilateral agreements and multilateral agreements. Here the multilateral agreements are only considered as they are more directly concerned with global environmental problems in accordance with the UN system. Tony Brenton has been critical of this type of classification of multilateral agreements and he argues that it is arbitrary one. According to him there are 64 international environmental agreements. In 1950 there were only six international environmental agreements while they increased to 11 in 1960, 26 in 1970 and 21 in 1980 (Brenton 1994). There are now hundreds of international environmental agreements, of which at least 120 are multilateral with contemporary relevance and some international legal substances (Vogler and Imber (Ed) 1996). However the major 51 international environmental agreements are examined and accordingly there are 38 conventions, eight agreements and five protocols. It reflects that there are more conventions and protocols than the agreements. Five of the 51 international environmental agreements have yet to come into force. In other words 10 per cent of the international environmental agreements have not been adopted (Field (1994).

There are two elements in the treaty: Primary and Secondary elements. Primary elements are those linked directly to object and purpose of international environmental agreements. The primary elements in the case of protecting the ozone layer will consist of strict rules for reducing emissions of ozone-depleting substances. Secondary elements will contribute to the realisation and application of the primary elements such as rules on compliance, state responsibility, trade restrictions, institutional arrangements and amendment procedures. There are three objectives that are aimed at in the treaty-making. First, it may codify measures to control environment. Second, it may form a precedent which can be applied elsewhere.

Third, it may turn the outcome of negotiations into a symbiosis of legal and scientific data, law provides the binding power. In the international environmental agreements, there are only eight agreements that have taken the shape of treaties which impose obligations on the parties in clear terms. Therefore there is the binding force of law. The remaining conventions and protocols including declarations are only soft laws which do not carry the force of law, but reflect political commitment on the part of governments. In fact making soft laws serves as the stepping stone towards more binding agreements.

There are certain conflicts and controversies that have been discussed in the earlier chapter on the sustainable development. It is difficult to reach a treaty immediately in the environmental issues. This can be achieved step by step. The first step is to start with the creation of a framework convention or umbrella treaty that broadly explains duties and areas of cooperation. Here more opportunities are provided for deliberations and debates. As soon as it is achieved, the second step would be to draft additional or supplementary protocols. The third step is leading to the formation of agreement that becomes the treaty.

Kinds

The agreements may be broadly divided into six kinds. They are marine pollution agreements, international river agreements, wildlife/habitat agreements, nuclear agreements, air pollution agreements, and miscellaneous agreements. There are eight major international environmental agreements of which the earliest is the International Convention for the Prevention of the Pollution of the Sea Oil, 1954, and it has come into force in 1958 with 75 signatories including the renouncing four nations. This agreement has the largest signatories. International Convention for the Prevention of Pollution from Ships, 1973, has yet to come into force even after the lapse of 23 years even though 19 nations attended the convention and signed. Agreement for cooperation in dealing with the pollution of the North Sea by oil came into force in 1969. Among the major agreements of this kind there is only one treaty and all others are conventions and protocols. In this kind of agreements it is revealed that the nations are reluctant to reach binding obligations. It can be stated that there is more preference for soft laws than the binding force of law.

In the second kind of agreements on international rivers there are four major agreements consisting of one treaty, one protocol, and two conventions. Here it is seen that the nations are more in favour of binding agreements. All the major agreements have come into force. Here the number of signatories are less than ten. Moreover this kind of agreement reveals that the importance of the water has made all the difference to the previous kind of agreements..

The third kind of agreements pertain to wildlife/habitat. There are 18 major agreements. The earliest major agreement was in 1902. There are two treaties and 16 protocols. The number of signatories to the agreements vary from 96 to 3. In this category one agreement is yet to come into force even after a lapse of 20 years. The reluctance of the nations to have binding agreements and the preference for the soft laws reveal the difficulty in reaching the agreements as every nation wants to exploit them despite knowing that it will result in environmental degradation.

There are five major agreements in nuclear field. There are two treaties and the remaining are conventions. The conventions relating to liability and the treaties are pertaining to banning the test and prohibition on use of weapons. Due to deterrent nuclear effect all the nations are ready to accept obligation. This is the achievement of human history. The credit goes to 20th century. The nations are reluctant to have binding agreements and they prefer the soft laws.

The fifth kind of agreements pertain to air pollution. There are six major agreements and all except one have come into force. There are four protocols, and two agreements are conventions without any treaty. In the recent 1996 Geneva Conference on Global Warming no agreement was reached on measures to reduce global warming. Despite having discovered depletion of ozone layer in 1984 and having understood the effect of global warming there is no agreement in preventing environmental degradation.

The sixth kind of agreements are miscellaneous in which there are ten agreements of which there are two treaties and three agreements are yet to come into force. The most important agreement which has not come into force is the Convention on the Law of the Sea since 1982 even though there are 161 signatories . It is the agreement that has the maximum number of signatories in the international environmental agreements.

Parties

The parties to international environmental agreements are playing a crucial role in concluding the agreements. This is facilitated through appropriate negotiation. This is one aspect of the issue. These parties may be divided into few categories. The first category is the parties who are involved as signatories. They are normally represented through their representatives of respective governments and these representatives may be civil servants. In the recently held convention on the Test Ban Treaty India vetoed the treaty and was done by a civil servant. The second kind of representatives may be the ministers representing the implementing governments. In the recently held Global Warming convention the ministers did not reach any consensus on most of the major issues. The third kind of representatives may be the representatives of the peoples and they may not be involved directly in the implementation process. The opposition party leader may be the representative in this kind. In this aspect the total number of signatories are the total parties to agreements. They play active role in concluding the agreements. In this aspect parties to agreements are influenced by certain factors that are vital to success of the convention or summit. National environmental policy, economic feasibility, geography, dependence on energy sources, nature and size of perceived threats and international status are some important factors. The treaty on Climate Change, 1992, has come into force immediately as soon as more than 160 signatories signed it. In the case of Treaty on Biodiversity even though the signatories have signed still the treaty has not come into force since 1992. United Nations conventions on the Law of the Sea 1982 have been signed by 161 signatories and till date it has not come into force effectively as many of the nations have not adopted it. At the same time there are only three signatories to the Convention on Conservation of Nature in the South Pacific 1976, and yet it has not come into force even after 20 years. Therefore the number of signatories are not the deciding factors for the conclusion of the treaty but in fact they are dictated by the issues that are mentioned above.

There is another aspect of the parties to agreements. Here the parties to agreements are not the parties who are implementing the agreements but they are assisting in the conclusion and coordination of the agreements. Assisting in the process are the experts, scientists, diplomats and mediators. There are parties who are participating in the assistance as well as coordination. These parties belong to international organisations under United Nations system, regional organisations, European Community, and non-government organisations.

Negotiation plays an important role in concluding agreements. To achieve a successful negotiation the following ingredients are essential:

1. to establish rules of the game that hold for formal dispute settlement;
2. to create a general framework for coordination of national policies;

3. to sustain platform for future negotiation; and
4. to develop a regime of confidence building that helps nations avoid open conflict (Sjostedt (Ed.) 1993).

There are four kinds of negotiations. The first is the traditional form of treaty negotiation in which there is common interest to all participants. The second kind of negotiation refers to joint measures to counteract a common threat like air pollution. In this type of negotiation the success depends upon the level of effective cooperation. Here is the problem of inadequate property rights which may lead the Tragedy of the Commons. The third kind of negotiation is based on the principles of altruism. Here there are more violations than strict compliance. However there are maximum number of agreements that are belonging to this kind of negotiation. Here there are more conventions than the agreements to bind the parties to agreements. The fourth kind of negotiation is belonging to ensuring a sustainable yield and regulating international trade in products obtained from natural resources.

CHAPTER 6

International Organisations

The international cooperation is an essential component in the enforcement of international environmental agreements and therefore it is appropriate to state that the international environmental law and international cooperation are complementary to each other. International environmental law needs an authority to supervise, control, regulate, and implement the international environmental agreements. In the absence of authority there is a vacuum in the implementation of international environmental law. This does not mean that the international environmental law is supplementary to international organisations. Every international organisation needs norms, a set of principles, and decision-making procedures around which actors' expectations converge in a given issue area as Krasner explains the regime. These instrumentalities are provided by the international environmental law (Vogler and Imber (Eds), 1996).Therefore, both are co-existent with each other. The international organisations and international environmental agreements are aiming to prevent environmental degradation, and to promote the conservation of natural resources (Boyle, 1991). The international organisations like UNO and other organisations under its system, World Bank, GATT/WTO, NGOs, and regional organisations are working towards the sustainable development and these will be discussed in this chapter.

The United Nations

UNO has been unilaterally assigned the responsibility of

promoting the sustainable development. This is evident in its contributions towards the sustainable development since 1972. Mark Imber attributes three reasons for it. First, the post-cold war UN provides a new impetus to the thrust on environmental issues. Secondly, because of its sustained efforts through conferences and other platforms of debates and deliberations, the South and North have recognised the explicit relationship between environmental degradation and patterns of economic development. Thirdly, the slogan for achieving sustainable development has become centre piece of UN activities similar to the decolonisation in the 1960s and the anti-aparthied in 1980s (Vogler and Imber (Eds) 1996). The UN performs basically two roles towards environment among other functions viz. an ***arena or forum*** for global bargaining between governments and an ***instrument*** for implementing and executing the policies of its members. UN organised the 1972 Stockholm Conference and the 1992 Rio Earth Summit. UN has facilitated the members to conclude more international environmental agreements. It has played a key role in diffusing tensions and conflicts between nations on environmental issues. These are some of the important functions that UN has performed under the first role. Establishment of the United Nations Environment Programme (UNEP) in 1972 and the Commission on Sustainable Development, represents one of the functions under the second role. UNEP is instrumental in creating the Global Environmental Facility in association with UNDP and World Bank and it has established the Global Environmental Monitoring System (GEMS) which helps member nations with environmental information while framing their national policies and for negotiations. Global Environmental Facility promotes the investment in projects towards sustainable development. UN has adopted the recommendations of World Conservation Strategy of ICUN in 1980, the Brundtland Report in 1987, and UNEP's Environmental Perspectives to the Year 2000 and Beyond in

1987. These recommendations have become global policies. UN Secretary-General has published the 'Agenda for Development' in 1994. To improve coordination among the 36 UN organs and 12 autonomous organisations, UNEP has established an Inter-Agency Task-Force on Environment and Development. The Commission on Sustainable Development was established in 1993 to coordinate UN activities on the environment and to monitor national and international implementation of Agenda 21 (Ken Canca 1995).

World Bank

World Bank and its affiliates, International Development Association, International Finance Corporation, and Multilateral Investment Agency, are actively involved in the realisation of sustainable development. World Bank group has singular responsibility of funding for poverty alleviation in the developing countries. Environment and development are conflicting to each other as it has been discussed in detail in the first chapter. Therefore the World Bank group has undertaken a policy change and structural change in their investment decisions and such changes took place in 1987. There are three factors responsible for these policy changes: the Brundtland Report 1987, the publication of the Development Committee Paper on Bank's Environment Strategy, and the appointment of Mr. Conable as the President of World Bank in 1987. World Bank has established a 'Standard Procedure for Environmental Assessment' to make investment decisions. 'Environment Issue Papers' on every borrower is prepared and it leads to the formation of 'National Environmental Action Plans' in the respective nations. To monitor them a separate ' Environment Department' under a vice -president, with four small regional 'Environment Units' in regions have been set up. Subsequently the American NGOs were prime movers in mobilising public and Congressional attention to the failure to pursue sound environmental practices, citing many examples of poverty-oriented World Bank projects with adverse environmental effects. During the Earth Summit 1992, a new vice-president for Environmental Sustainable Development was appointed. Now there are six Regional Environmental Divisions under six regional vice-presidents. New Environmental Strategy was published in 1992 in World Development Report consisting of win-win policies like removal of subsidies, water and sanitation infrastructure and so on. The new environmental strategy proposes market oriented policy reforms and institutional reforms. These policies are reoriented in the lending programmes. Moreover the lending programmes are in line with the Agenda 21 of Earth Summit (Mahbub (Ed.) 1995). Since 1994 the World Bank has adopted the following four-fold agenda in its policy decisions and programmes to:

1. help member nations set priorities, build institutions, and implement programmes for sound environmental stewardship;
2. ensure that potential adverse environmental impacts from Bank-financed projects are addressed;
3. help member countries build on the connections among poverty reduction, economic efficiency, and environmental protection; and to
4. address global environmental challenges through participation in the Global Environmental Facility (World Bank 1994)

GATT/WTO

A General Agreement on Tariff and Trade was concluded in 1947, as an interim measure with the hope of getting it replaced by international agency under UN system, in order to remove barriers and promote free and open World Trading System. An International Trading Organisation was considered as an international agency to replace the GATT but it died unborn. In January 1995, the World Trading Organisation

(WTO) replaced the GATT after it had concluded eight Negotiating Rounds of which the Eighth Round, known as the Uruguay Round held between 1986 and 1994, was directly responsible for the establishment of WTO.

There is no specific provision in the WTO Agreement on environmental sustainability in international trade except a passing remark in the Preamble. However in the Uruguay Round it was agreed to constitute a new committee on Trade and Environment to identify the relationship between trade measures for promoting sustainable development, and on their recommendations, appropriate modifications will be incorporated in the multilateral trading system. GATT (Article XX) allows certain unilateral trade measures towards environmental protection. The paragraph 2.2 of agreement on Technical Barriers to Trade encourages international harmonisation of product standards towards environmental protection. There are certain international environmental agreements that impose trade restraints, among others, such as Montreal Protocol on ozone-depleting chemicals, Basel conventions on Transboundary movements of hazardous wastes, and convention on international trade in endangered species of wild fauna and flora (CITES) (Field, 1994).

NGOs

Environmental non-governmental organisations have contributed significantly in promoting sustainable development through helping, assisting, bargaining, and coordinating with international organisations both locally and globally. The NGOs are proliferating faster than ever before since the Stockholm Conference. Before the Stockholm Conference the NGOs had been playing a very limited role within the United Nations unlike at the present. The UNESCO has been instrumental in the establishment of International Union for the Conservation of Nature (ICUN). The World Wildlife Fund for Nature (WWF) became the first fund raising NGO in 1961.

The ICUN prepared the World Charter for Nature, and the United Nations adopted it in 1982. It had also prepared and adopted the World Conservation Strategy, 1980, which is beginning for the development of the concept of sustainable development in the Brundtland Report, 1987. WWF has 23 representatives of national organisations of developed and developing nations. One of the principle activities of the WWF is financing operations of conservation throughout the world. WWF and ICUN prepare annually a common strategy for financing programmes towards conservation leading to sustainable development (Alexander and Dinesh, 1991). WWF and Greenpeace enjoy greater access to UN deliberations. Other influential environmental NGOs are World Resource Institute, Worldwatch Institute, International Institute for Environment, the Centre for Our Common Future, the Third World Network, and the Independent Sectors Network. About 1000, 1400 and 550 NGOs are accredited to UNESCO, UNEP, and Commission on Sustainable Development respectively. It is believed 1600 NGOs had participated in the NGO Global Forum during the Earth Summit, 1992. There are 200,000 grassroot NGOs including 30000 grass support organisations (Ken Conca, 1995).

Regional Organisations

The regional organisations have also grown in pace with the global organisations. In Europe there are many regional organisations on environment. A few factions are relevant to mention on the growth of regional organisations in Europe. First, Europe is very densely populated and highly industrialised, leading to greater risks of environmental deterioration. Second, the process of political and legal integration is most developed in Europe. Third, cooperation in environmental matters is facilitated by the homogeneity of economic and political systems especially in Western Europe.

The oldest regional organisation is the United Nations

Economic Commission for Europe (UNECE) which was created in 1947 by the UNESCO. The UNECE is basically providing analytical, economic, technological and statistical information to governments. It has 34 member countries from Western and Central Europe and North America. Since 1956, its contribution has become very prominent. In 1963, a committee was appointed to look into the problems of air pollution in coal factories, heating plants and thermal pollution of inland waters. In 1971, it created a principal subsidiary organ for the cause of environment. It has helped in concluding several international environmental agreements and also played an important role in the promotion of international environmental law. The Council of Europe is the oldest existing European institution. It was created in London May 5, 1949. It has 25 member states consisting of Western and Central Europe, of which 12 are part of European Economic Community. In 1962, it created an European Committee for Protection of Nature and Natural Resources. The Council has adopted European Water Charter, 1968, and the Soil Charter, 1972. It has created numerous legislative documents on various aspects of environment and these have become part of international environmental law. Another important regional organisation is the Organisation of Economic Co-operation and Development, 1960, which is the successor of the Organisation of European Economic Co-operation founded in 1948. It created a Committee on Environment in 1970 with a purpose of assisting its members states to define their policies on environmental problems and to reconcile their environmental policies with economic and social development. It has contributed more in the growth of international environmental agreements and international environmental law through declarations, principles, and definitions of pollution applicable to trans-frontier pollution. The other important regional organisations are European Communities, Conference on Security and Co-operation in

Europe (CSCE), Organisation of American States (OAS), South Pacific Commission, International Boundary and Water Commission and International Joint Commission.

CHAPTER 7

Enforcement and Participation

International environmental law aims, among other objectives, at promoting sustainable development. International environmental law consists of the substantive, procedural and institutional rules of international law with the primary objective of environmental protection (Sands, 1995). The legal definition of the environment is essential for two reasons: to identify the impact of and areas of natural resources that may become subject to environmental degradation, and to define the competence of international organisations to seek enforcement through courts of law or as a party to international agreements and their compliance. For example, the non-availability of a proper definition of 'whale' has led to inconclusive disputes on the enforcement of 1946 International Whaling Convention. Again the conditions that are controlled, may become a 'non-natural environment' where artificially propagated plants are grown. Such essential features are essential to establish liability for damage. Philippe Sands argues that the international law of sustainable development is broader than international environmental law since the limitations of legal definition of environment do not apply to international law where social, political and economic definitions of sustainable development are liberally and widely applied. Professor Gerd Winter argues that all law is environmental law because the history of environment is the history of mankind and law. Therefore there is no distinction between international law and international environmental law. Prof. Weiss says that the international environmental law permeates beyond international law. Agreeing with Prof. Weiss, Lothar Gundling states that the principles of environmental law have become part and parcel of national and international laws. Broadly speaking both international law and international environmental law may look different, but they are both concerned with sustainable development. Enforcement of international environmental law relies on international actors like international organisations and non-governmental organisations. Participation of international organisations in international environmental agreements with other parties may help in compliance, implementation and enforcement. These issues will be briefly discussed in this chapter.

Enforcement of Environmental Agreements

Enforcement has three aspects viz. compliance, implementation, and enforcement. Compliance means avoiding non-compliance with international environmental agreements. Non-compliance happens under six conditions largely. Normally, first the states enter into innumerable international agreements including environmental agreements. It becomes hard to implement each international obligation all the time. Often, it happens that the casualty is environmental. Secondly, it is due to the growing demands for exploitation of natural resources to meet the needs of growth and development as there is no clear property right. Thirdly, there are certain finite natural resources which do not have substitutes or for which the cost of recycling is too high or there is no technology available. Fourthly, the lack of proper technology may cause mismanagement of natural resources. Or it may be due to underdevelopment: there is no technology. Fifthly, international environmental obligations increasingly intersect with economic interests, and states which do not comply with environmental obligations are perceived to gain economic advantage from non-compliance. Sixth, the inadequacies in the enforcement mechanism hardly bring any consequential differences between compliance and non-compliance.

There are three theories that explain the causes for non-compliance with international environmental obligations and these are the 'Tragedy of the Commons', 'Prisioner's Dilemma', and Olson's the 'Logic of Collective Action'. Hardin has developed the theory of the Tragedy of the Commons. It explains the free-rider problem which is due to free and open-access. Each one wants to maximise his benefit. Moreover every one may shirk his responsibility. According to this principle the economic cost is shifted to social or group costs. The free-rider behaviour is assumed to be the dominant motive against which the group is defenceless. Natural resource mismanagement leads to environmental degradation as there is dominant motive for non-compliance of international environmental obligations. Another principle explaining the non-compliance is the Prisioner's Dilemma which offers the choice between compliance and non-compliance. As there is no liability on non-compliance every nation attempts non-compliance with international environmental obligations. The third principle is the Multiperson Prisioner's Dilemma (MPD). This principle explains multiple choices of compliance and non-compliance. If the majority cooperates there is maximum benefit. If there is non-compliance still there is gain and others may also benefit. These are illustrated in the diagrams given on next page.

The vertical axis in diagrams A and B shows the pay-off to compliance by nations **(n+1)** to international environmental agreements when certain number of nations choose compliance and others choose non-compliance. The upper curve **NC** denotes dominant choice of non-compliance and the curve **C** denotes the choice of compliance. Where **k=n**, no

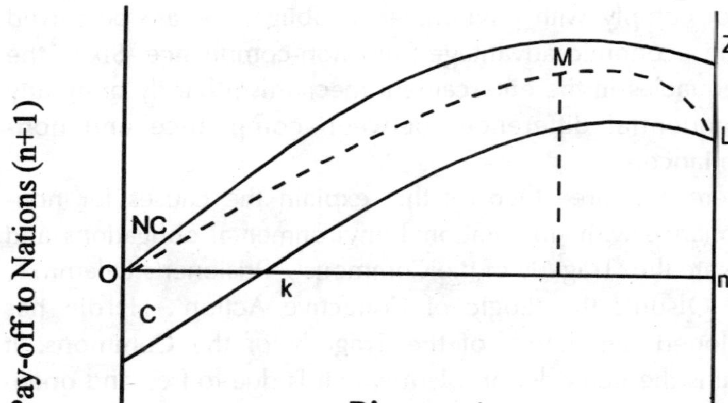

Diagram A

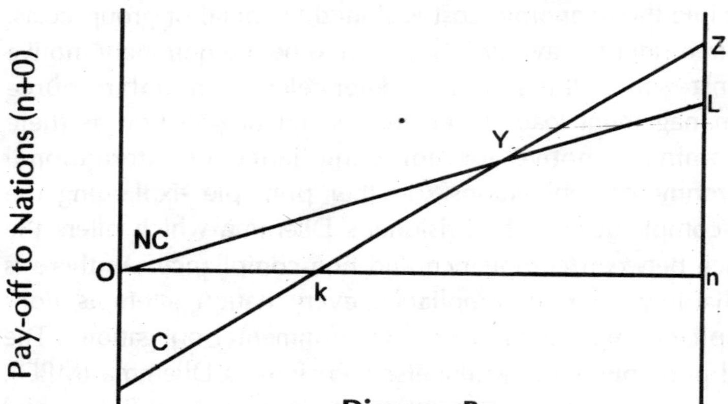

Diagram B

Source : Corlisle Ford Runge, 1986

one gains from compliance unless compliance is universal and there are no free-riders. Where **k<n**, some free-riders **(n-k)** can be tolerated while k nations , who comply, gain even though free-riders **(n-k)** benefit more than the nations who comply. **O** shows the open access equilibrium in which no nations comply and rents are driven to zero. **M** denotes the maximum collective gain.

In the MPD model every nation has an incentive to free-ride resulting in over-exploitation of natural resources and environmental degradation. Every nation is of the view that with non-compliance one gains more. In the MPD model of compliance these observations lead to: an inferior outcome; a dominant free-rider strategy; and a need for enforcement (Runge 1986). Mancur Olson's theory proposes that voluntary collective action will not produce public goods and collective action based on selective and positive or negative incentives may produce public goods.

The 'assurance problem' by A. Sen, 'coordination problem' by Shilling have been suggested as an alternative to the model of MPD. In both these cases minimum enforcement is required. Alternatively, by removing the free-rider motive under the conditions of necessity of survival or extinction there will be successful compliance. It is illustrated below:

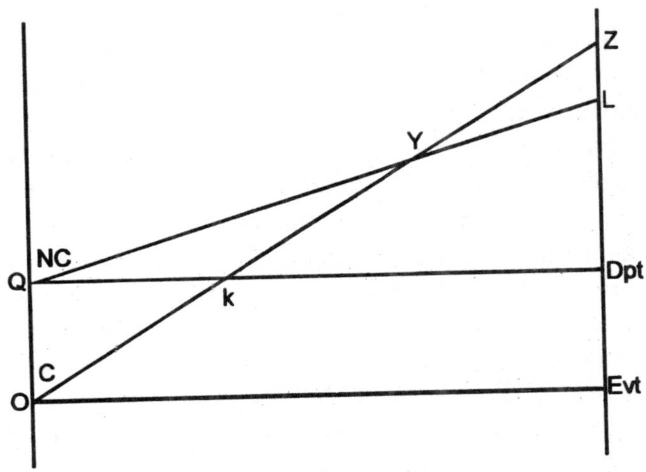

Diagram C

Number of other nations choosing the compliance

Keeping the explanations as referred to in the Diagrams A and B, here the maximum compliance and the superior equilibrium are achieved at **Z** since compliance is more beneficial than non-compliance as the **NC** reaches an inferior equilibrium at **L.**

The next stage of enforcement is implementation which is carried out in three ways. Implementation is carried out by adopting national implementing measures. This has different forms. First, it can incorporate the obligations into national legislation. If the treaty obligations are not domestically implemented, there will be difficulty in enforcing them in national courts. However EC law provides an exception to this rule in the enforcement of international obligations in the national courts. The second form of implementation is by ensuring that national measures are complied with by those subject to their jurisdiction and control. Art. 15 (1) of 1972 Oslo Convention, Art. VIII (1) of 1973 CITES, and, Art. 12 of 1974 Paris Convention, expressly, have provisions to ensure compliance. There are certain treaties like 1982 UN Convention on the Law of Sea which allocate enforcement obligations to particular states. The Climate Change Convention requires the developed countries to incur the costs in complying with international obligations by the developing countries. The third form of implementation is the fulfilment of obligations to international organisations such as reporting the measures taken to give effect to international obligations. For example, the United States General Accounting Office reports on variations in compliance of reporting among the treaties (Sands 1995).

The next stage of the enforcement is the 'enforcement' itself. The compliance and implementation are internally managed to enforce the international environmental obligations. The 'enforcement' here is achieved externally. Enforcement denotes the right to take measures for the fulfilment of international environmental obligations, or to obtain a ruling from any appropriate international court, tribunal or other body, including an international organisation. The action for enforcement may be initiated by one or more states, or any international organisation or by non-governmental actors. It is possible either by any one of them, or by all of them. States have the primary role in enforcing rules of international environmental law. A state must prove that it has *locus standi* or standing as 'injured state', according to Art. 5 of International Law Commission's Draft Articles on State Responsibility. In cases of claiming environmental damage, there are two aspects. First, it is the damage that is caused within the state by another state. Secondly, it pertains to the damage caused by another state outside the jurisdiction of a state. In the first respect, for example, in the case of the Trail Smeller case, the United States invoked its rights not to be subjected to trans-boundary air pollution from sulphur emissions in Canada and to bring a claim against Canada for having violated its rights. In the second aspect, in the Nuclear Test case, Australia and New Zealand claimed against France to halt its atmospheric nuclear testing in the South Pacific region (Sands 1995).

The enforcement action brought by international organisations is limited even though their legislative role in bringing international environmental agreements is immense. International organisations are international legal persons and they play an important role in enforcement.. However, to enforce international environmental obligations, the enforcement actions may be brought, with their consent, for the benefit of other states also, or it may be for the benefit of all. Normally, the sovereign interests of the states have become a constraint to the transfer of more enforcement power to international organisations. For example Art. 12 (1) of 1958 Danube Fishing Convention, and Art. XI (5) of 1978 Northwest Atlantic Fisheries Convention of Salmon in the North Atlantic Ocean, have transferred limited power of enforcement to international organisations. However, the trend towards transferring more enforcement power to international organisations is visible in the recent international environmental agreements like 1982 UN Convention on Law of Sea. Art. 162 of 1982 UN Convention on Law of Sea empowers the Council of the International Sea-Bed Authority to supervise and coordinate the implementation and report to the Assembly if there is any non-compliance specified in Part XI. According to Art. 165 (2) (i) and (j), the Legal and Technical Commission, one of the Council's organs, will be entitled to make recommendations to the Council on the institution of proceedings and if any measure is taken as a result of the decision by the Sea-Bed Disputes Chamber. Similar powers are provided in the 1992 OPSAR Convention under Art. 23.

In the traditional rules of the public international law, non-governmental actors are not recognised as international legal persons except within the limited role confining to international human rights law and its associated field. (*ibid*). However in practice, the non-governmental actors play an important role in the implementation of international environmental agreements at national level, through political means or by recourse to administrative or judicial procedures. Chapter 27:13 of Agenda 21 and Principle 10 of Rio Declaration of UNCED 1992, the non-governmental actors are empowered to have a stronger role in enforcing international environmental laws and obligations before national courts and tribunals.

Often if there is failure in the fulfilment of international environmental obligations it is due to a failure of enforcement. This will lead to disputed claims and thus there is a provision for international conflict resolution (Settlement of Disputes) so as to achieve enforcement of international environmental agreements. There are well established procedures and mechanisms, including negotiation, enquiry, mediation, conciliation, arbitration, judicial settlement, and resort to regional agencies or arrangements, or other means of the parties' own choice. Arbitration and judicial settlement may form the legal means to settle disputes. These decisions are binding. Other mechanisms of dispute settlement are known as diplomatic means of settlement of disputes. Initially the environmental agreements proposed only non-binding and informal means of dispute settlement. Now the trend is changing. The 1992 Climate Change Convention has proposed three mechanisms: a Subsidiary Body for implementation, Multilateral Consultative Process, and thirdly, the settlement of disputes in more traditional ways by negotiation or the ICJ, or international conciliation.

Problems

There are certain problems which are responsible for the non-implementation of international environmental agreements. Some of them are associated with the nature of international environmental agreements; some of them are due to the slow growth of international environmental law; a few of them are due to weak organisational structure of international organisations; and some of them are inherent in the role of non-governmental actors. According to Art. 38 of the International Court of Justice, the sources which decide the order of enforceability of international law are treaties, customs, and general principles established by law. Most of the international environmental agreements are conventions, protocols, and declarations which are not recognised sources of international law. Therefore there is less scope for enforcement. In the initial stage the member states proposed a stronger role for international organisation and they agreed to transfer enforcement power to them. But, later they chose not to transfer enforcement power. In the case of 1988 CRAMRA, initially, the Antarctic Mineral Resource Commission would have enforcement power, but in the final stage of concluding the convention, the enforcement role of the Commission modified to a mere advisory role in the 1991 Protocol (ibid).

Absence of legally binding provisions in the international environmental agreements is a cause for the failure of enforcement in the national courts and at national level. The Philippines has decided to exploit geothermal power near the Mt. Apo National Park even though it is prohibited in the ASEAN Declaration on Heritage Site and Reserve. No action could be brought against the decision. There are certain inconsistencies between global agreements and national practices resulting failure of implementation in accordance with international environmental agreements. The first inconsistency is the principle of sovereignty which is recognised by the UNO: every sovereign state has an inherent right to exploit its natural resources for development. International environmental agreements aim to regulate exploitation which amounts to an interference in the sovereignty. The second inconsistency is the right to development adopted at the 1992 Earth Summit. The developing nations pursue economic growth using the natural resources and they try to justify their refusal to curb their growth options as the industrialised nations are responsible for the present environmental degradation. It is also argued that the UNO is biased towards North in the shaping of international environmental agreements (ibid).

Consequences

The act of signing an international environmental agreement remains a political event without impact if there is no implementation. There is a quantitative increment in the growth of international environmental agreements lacking qualitative significance. The enforcement is diluted as much as possible so as to make it non-existent. Environmental degradation flourishes unabated. Acidification of Swedish lakes due to CO_2 emissions from coal burning in Britain, and other fossil fuel emissions, is an example. Specific use of natural resources causes deterioration to other states' natural resources and the planet as a whole. The effect of global warming, reported recently in England, is expected to affect her rainfall and temperature severely within a decade. Forest burning in tropical regions contributes to the causes of the greenhouse gas effect. According to FAO' report, shifting cultivation is the cause for the loss of 70 per cent forest in Africa, 50 per cent in Asia, and 35 per cent in America. It is feared that the tropical forests will disappear in AD 2040 if the present trend of annual clearance of 169,000 km, continues (Kirkby (Ed.) 1996). The loss of biodiversity could not be controlled despite innumerable agreements, and in fact, the earliest of all is dated to 1902. The industrialised countries account for 80 per cent of world-wide cumulative emission of CO2 during the period of 1950-86. The depletion of ozone layer continues to remain a concern without much progress. The reduction of CFC is not yet achieved. Therefore, it is very difficult to share out the responsibility for coping with the impacts of climate change, as also for keeping the collective environmental pressures of 10 billion people within tolerable limits (Grubb, 1995).

There is a need for a total review of the enforcement of international environmental agreements and for strengthening international environmental law.

Participation in Environmental International Agreements

The proposal of Sweden to discuss environmental issues in 1968, in the Economic and Social Council, was the beginning of international cooperation and participation in international environmental agreements formally. There are various reports on the total number of international environmental agreements. It is reported that there are 180 agreements, and according to another report there are 120 agreements (Harris 1996 and Vogler and Imber 1996). Haas, Keohane and Levy have estimated that there have been 140 international environmental agreements since 1921 and more than half of them have been concluded since the 1972 Stockholm Conference (Bernauer 1995). There are various estimates of the number of agreements but the fact remains that participation in international environmental agreements has increased consistently since the Stockholm Conference which has recognised the importance of international cooperation through active participation. It is evident that the nine principles (11, 12, 19, 20, 22, 23, 24, 25, & 26) of the 26 principles speak for international cooperation. In the 1992 Earth Summit, special provisions were incorporated in Agenda 21 which would encourage the participation of Third World countries in the promotion of international cooperation so as to bring more international environmental agreements. Regional organisations like the European Community have played important role in promoting participation of member states to conclude more international environmental agreements.

To achieve effective participation, effective negotiation is essential. The consent of states to participate in negotiation is the beginning, and to accept the proposals of international environmental agreements is the conclusion of negotiation, including ratification. International organisations have provided the initiatives and venues for negotiation.

Problems

The North-South gap has been a constant impediment to the effective participation as discussed in the earlier chapters. The lack of funding is one of the causes for the inability of Global Environmental Monitoring System to provide sufficient information on environmental issues. Due to paucity of funds, the UNEP finds difficult to carry out the task of spreading environmental education, and institutional support of scientific and technological research are the main victims. The Third

World countries remain isolated for want of environmental information and funds including the problems of balance of payments and debts. The promises of financial transfers through aid and grants have not materialised but have rather remained only words. Lack of definite property rights has encouraged defection, known as free-rider problem and lack of incentives and authority as discussed in the Tragedy of the Commons and the Logic of Collective Action. According to the Prisioner's Dilemma the member states tend to avoid co-operation as less the international environmental obligations less the risk of loss.

Consequences

Lack of participation has resulted in mismanagement of natural resources and environmental degradation. Most of the international environmental agreements have not become agreements that are legally enforceable. These agreements are mere protocols and conventions which do not have legal sanctity except a moral constraint which can always be violated on various reasons.

Performance Appraisal of International Organisations

Primarily there are three problems in the performance of international organisations:

— environmental issues are inherently complex,
— each institution has several goals including environmental, and
— there are certain dependent and exogenous variables which make the assessment inaccurate. (Bernauer 1995). A brief assessment will be made of these constraints here.

International organisations are instrumental in providing a platform and opportunities to discuss and deliberate environmental issues. UN Economic and Social Council has played this role effectively since 1968 focusing on the proposal of Sweden on environmental issues to the UNO which led to the organisation of the 1972 Stockholm Conference and 1992 Earth Summit. Some of the important international actions would be worth mentioning such as the establishment of UNEP, Global Environmental Monitoring System as a result of the Stockholm Conference, establishment of a Network of Biosphere Reserves in 1976 by UNESCO, creation of the International Register of Potentially Toxic Chemicals in 1976, establishment of Global Environmental Facility in 1990, signature campaign of 'Earth Pledge' in 1991, and the establishment of the Commission of Sustainable Development. By virtue of these actions and setting up of the institutions there has been a positive impact on negotiation and participation (UN Chronicle 1992).

The UN system is able to undertake collection, interpretation and dissemination of large scale data through World Weather Watch, CITES and GEMS so as to facilitate negotiation and international cooperation. The UN system has been instrumental in evolving consensus negotiation norms such as common heritage principles, demilitarisation of sea-bed and the moon and outer space. It is able to ensure safeguards and inspection regimes to monitor compliance with treaties such as the IAEA safeguards and the Montreal Protocol (Imber 1993). The OECD has contributed important principles such as the polluter pays principle, the precautionary principle, and the principle of subsidiarity to the international environmental law. NGOs have established a link between national and international bodies to achieve and promote implementation of international environmental obligations. International organisations have achievements in confidence building among the nations and their collective participation role in protecting the environment in contrast to the traditional method of enforcing international environmental law. The traditional method of enforcing the obligation is to impose sanctions or suspend the defaulting nations. In this method the nations are motivated to participate, and the international organisation achieves the implementation through cooperation. The UN has developed techniques and systems for political supervision and regulation. The European Convention on Human Rights and Inter-American Human Rights Convention employ supervisory commissions. The International Court of Justice has confirmed the regulatory and supervisory role of UN in the Namibia Advisory Opinion (Boyle 1991).

The World Bank modified its policies and priorities in 1987 to suit the needs of sustainable development. It approves the projects with a system of environmental assessment and supports member countries with National Environmental Action Plans. The Bank works closely with UNEP, UNDP, and its allies through the Global Environmental Facility which has emerged as an important catalyst for integrating global environmental concerns into national development goals, with a special emphasis on developing countries role in global warming, biological diversity, protection of international river systems and the prevention of depletion of the ozone layer (Mahabub (Ed.) 1995 and World Bank 1994). United Nations Development Programme is at the centre of the UN development system of funding and technical cooperation. UNDP has launched a Capacity 21 Fund with $ 100 million to assist developing countries towards sustainable development through their socio-economic plans and programmes. UNEP has contributed immensely to the growth of international environmental law. International organisations have proved effective in peaceful settlements of international environmental disputes (Sjostedt (Ed.) 1993).

The World Conservation Strategy of 1980, ICUN, Environmental Perspective to the year 2000 and Beyond, 1987, of UNEP, the Sustainable Development of the WCED , 1987, and World Charter of Nature, 1982, have contributed valuable concepts and policies towards international cooperation on environmental issues and international environmental law in its application (Redclift 1987, Adams 1990, UN Year 1987, and Alexander and Shelton 1991).

Problems

The most important problem with the UN system is the weak coordination of integrated programmes involving many agencies singly engaged in sectoral work. The second problem is the lack of taxation and other financial measures creating incentives for responsible environmental behaviour of member states. The third shortcoming is the inability to impose sanctions against errant states and to sustain sanctions. The fourth problem is the capacity to openly criticise and reprimand members in violation of norms and rules and the power to sustain it (Imber 1993). These problems refer to lack of 'authority' and 'incentives' as pointed out in Olson's the Logic of Collective Action applied to common property management. The fifth problem is the isolation of environmental issues between North and South. Michael Grubb argues that the climate change is likely to kill more poor people than rich people, and the ultimate benefit is likely to be greatest for the developing countries (Grubb 1995). This encourages the free-rider motive of one group over others in the management of common resources. Sixth, the lack of implementation of promises contained in the polluter pays principle and common but discriminated responsibilities has failed to motivate the Third World countries to participate in the international cooperation. Seventh, the paucity of funds is the biggest challenge before international organisations.

Consequences

Due to non-implementation and failure to pursue the basic tenets of sustainable development enshrined in international environmental agreements, the apprehensions stated violently in the 'Limit to Growth', 'Beyond the Limit' and 'End of the World' are becoming evident that 'over the long term, species extinction cannot exceed species evolution; soil erosion cannot exceed soil formation; forest destruction cannot exceed forest regeneration, carbon emissions cannot exceed carbon fixation; fish catches cannot exceed the regenerative capacity of fisheries; and human births cannot exceed human deaths (Brown 1994).

CHAPTER 8

Conclusion

Daniel C' Esty, after analysing the existing organisational structure on environmental issues to overcome 'adhocism', and 'too many cooks', suggests the establishment of a separate global agency known as the Global Environmental Organisation, for three reasons, viz., to address global environmental issues exclusively, to promote shared learning in addressing common environmental problems, and to reduce competitiveness, tensions and to assist member nations on environmental policy decisions. This suggestion unfortunately has failed to meet the complex environmental issues which need active participation and positive cooperation of the community of nations in the pursuit of sustainable development. A single institution irrespective of its size and competence cannot deal with the environmental issues in isolation as the development is equally involved. Owen Greene raises the criticism that these institutions are established through a process of compromise amongst national and international policy-makers who have at best only a partial understanding of the external environment. International organisations are subject to patterns of power, interest, influence, capacity, and commitment to development. Moreover many international environmental conventions fail to have legal obligations (Vogler and Imber (Ed.)- 1996). The global environmental norms such as generality of participation, external and internal diplomacy, flexibility and speciality do not prevent defection and violation, according to Roderick Ogley.

These are the views which narrate the reasons for improvements and not rejections. International environmental law has been able to emerge slowly but steadily under the patronage of the existing international organisations. The whole community of nations have recognised all the principles of international environmental law even though there are some differences among the nations in accepting totally certain principles like the polluter pays and the inter-generational principle. Criticisms are to identify the shortcomings so as to initiate suitable measures. In the 1992 Earth Summit , NGOs' role is recognised; the need for assistance to developing nations in the promotion of sustainable development is recognised in Agenda 21; and the importance of internationa environmental agreements is endorsed. Therefore there is a need to strengthen existing organisations to achieve sustainable development through active international cooperation and positive implementation of international environmental agreements and acceptance of the principles of international environmental law. In this chapter the measures to strengthen them and empowerment of sustainable development will be briefly discussed.

Strengthening International Agreements

International environmental agreements should be used as potent tools for influencing policies at national level. For example Nepal has passed suitable legislation and mace amendments despite the compelling need for development which needs exploitation of natural resources. It has identified the areas where there has to be strict legislation to prohibit further exploitation of natural resources (Krishna Prasad Oli 1996). Many of the Third World countries like Somalia, Burundi, etc., have not achieved the political stability which is essential to enforce international environmental obligations at national level. To overcome this problem, the regional arrangements have to be strengthened as in the case of

European Community and ASEAN. In single EC law the member states need not have separate domestic legislation to enforce international environmental obligations in the national courts. Therefore the international organisations must encourage such regional arrangements among member states.

There should be sufficient decentralisation of authority at regional level so as to achieve both peaceful means and legal means of settlement of disputes. In addition, regional agreements should be encouraged among the member states as seen in the OECD. Susskind and Ozawa have made nine recommendations to improve the convention and protocol approach of international environmental agreements. These include empowering non-traditional clusters of countries to caucus well ahead of formal negotiations, encouraging poor countries to participate, developing multiple proposals, expanding the role of NGOs, reviewing the application of the discriminated responsibility principle, improving access to information on environmental issues, encouraging appropriate linkages between environment and development, encouraging unilateral actions and finally involving the mass-media in negotiations (Susskind and Ozawa 1992). Some of these recommendations had been considered in UNCLOS III. The result is not encouraging as UNCLOS has come into force in November 1994 in a different shape to the original proposal. (Vogler and Imber (Ed) 1996). Thus, in addition to the above it is suggested that there shall be an inbuilt mechanism to incorporate an enforcement action plan in phases so as to identify the practical points of disagreements on the implementation before reaching a final agreement within the stipulated time framework. This will ensure that there is scope for enforcement of international environmental obligations.

The right to environment and development have to be made enforceable fundamental rights or civil rights so that the violations by respective nations will be held responsible. This will remove the problem of *locus standi*.

Strengthening International Organisations

Interaction among thirty-six UN organs and twelve specialised agencies needs to be improved so as to achieve better co-ordination among the NGOs and regional organisations. The World Bank and other developmental agencies should be given a definite definition of development which is missing now. This is evident in the report of Agenda for Development. In this report, after detailed discussions in General Assembly after two years of preparations unlike six months in the case of Agenda for Peace, the Secretary-General has made his recommendations for revitalising international development cooperation, an effective multilateral development system, and more effective and efficient UN developmental activities. (Rivlin 1995)

To facilitate active participation and cooperation among the member states international institutions should increase transparency, reduce uncertainty, mediate disputes, and provide procedures for aggregating individual choices at lower cost (Bernauer 1995). This will ensure confidence in the member countries that they are part of the activities.

To overcome the problems of Prisioner's Dilemma, the Tragedy of the Commons and the Logic of Collective Action, the stable cooperative equilibrium is suggested. In the stable cooperative equilibrium, no actor has incentives to defect no matter what the other actors do. (ibid). These suggestions do not find favour in practice, as the North-South gap makes these suggestions inoperative. Therefore there should be constructive efforts to bridge the gap between North and South through negotiation, diplomacy, conference, financial aid and assistance constructively without such conditionalities which amount to interference in their domestic policies and without infringing their sovereignty. Ultimately India and China agreed to sign the Montreal Protocol in 1992, and to reduce CFC emissions from 1995 onwards. And a close monitoring between growth and development will reduce the gap between

North and South and achieve sustainable development, with proper coordination and cooperation. Harold Brookefield has analysed various options to rationalise the mismanagement of natural resources after examining the principles of the Hotelling Rule, Hartwick Rule, Cake-eating, and 'keeping capital intact' including the populist ideologies of Robert Chambers (1984), Richards (1985), and the World Conservation Strategy, and finally concludes that the willingness by governments to put social priorities with a special thrust to the environment and active support by the global public to them are essential (Stokke (Ed) 1991). The global polices that are pursued by international organisations and national policies adopted by the member nations must be complementary to each other and not supplementary to each other. At the same time insurance for future generations should not be left only to the principle of inter-generational equity and the ethical constraint (Slow 1991), but it should also be in the national Social Charter of every nation which is endorsed by the member states in association with international organisations.

Empowerment of Sustainable Development

The contradictions and controversies in the concept of sustainable development have to be removed. It is also true that the concept of sustainable development is dynamic and not static. A one time solution will not ever remove the contradictions and controversies and therefore persistent efforts in this direction are essential. As the humanity survives the sustainaibility survives. The end of humanity is the end of sustainable development. Both are inseparable. There may be a degree of variation in each stage of history. This understanding has to emerge among us with unanimity. The delay in unanimity is the delay in understanding. Therefore it is the embodiment of collective wisdom. It will be unwise to split it beyond a limit. The 'Limits to the Growth', 'Beyond the

Limit' and 'The End of the World' including the 'Without the End of the World' are the aberrations of collective wisdom. The loss of life is the loss of humanity and that of sustainable development. Therefore it needs to be strengthened and there should be empowerment where there is inequality, poverty, and discrimination. Exploitation is the root cause of all these miseries. Utility is one thing and exploitation is another. Exploitation leads to deprivation of others. None is endowed with the right to exploit denying to others including future generations. This is the important factor which holds the truth of the free-rider problem. Unless the exploitation is stopped the free-rider problem cannot be solved. The poverty of collective wisdom is the cause of the free-rider problem. Lack of collective wisdom is the problem of international cooperation. As long as the inequality is allowed to flourish, the implementation of international environmental agreements is the embodiment of disillusion and imagination.

To achieve it , it is suggested that there shall be total participation in the management of natural resources. If all the nations choose to participate in the international environmental agreements, the mismanagement of the natural resources may be removed and the environmental degradation avoided. This will ensure sustainable development. To achieve this the free-rider problem has to be eliminated. The North and South gap is to be removed. The removal of the gap between them will be the incentive to the South to participate in the compliance of the international environmental obligations. International organisations will be able to ensure it through the developmental institutions like World Bank, United Nations Development Programme, International Monetary Fund, and other regional arrangements. The 'Agenda for Development' has to be sincerely implemented. The developed nations must also allocate a percentage of per capita income for the development of South.

This is illustrated in the following diagrams:

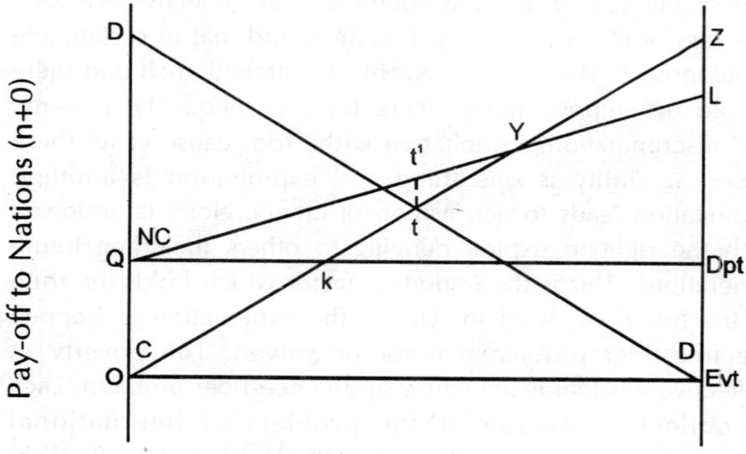

Diagram D

Number of other nations choosing the compliance

OQ axis shows the pay-off to the nations on compliance. **NC** curve denotes the number of nations choosing the non-compliance and the **C** curve is for the compliance by number of nations. **Dpt** is the line which denotes the development and the **Evt** is for the environment. From the point of view of present day developed nations, the nations choosing compliance do not have the option of non-compliance as these nations have tremendous environmental stress. Moreover these nations have already achieved development and they can afford to have limited-growth. This is happening with North where annual growth is almost stagnated at 2 per cent while the developing nations are around 3.5 per cent for the same period. As the demand is more for development the South tends to prefer development. Therefore there is more non-compliance as shown in the curve **NC** and there is less scope for achieving sustainable development.

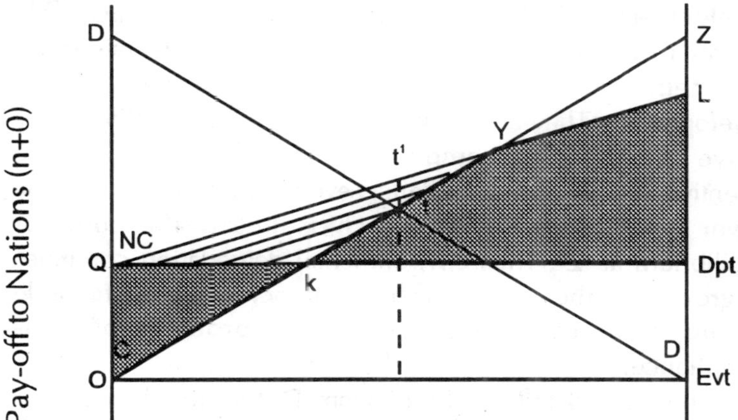

Diagram E

Number of other nations choosing the compliance

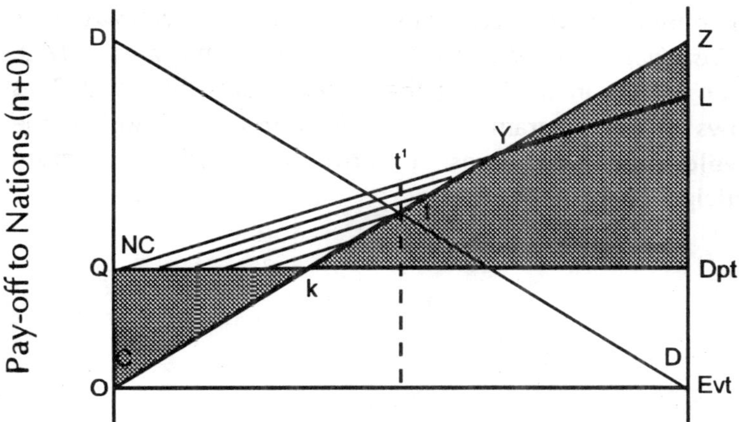

Diagram F

Number of other nations choosing the compliance

Keeping other details of the previous diagram D as discussed above, in the diagram E, the **D curve** shows the demand for development due to poverty and underdevelopment in Third World countries. As they have only natural resources, since they lack capital and technology , they tend to exploit more natural resources for the development. They are achieving a gain of **'t'** to **'t^1'** which is above the point of compliance. Therefore they get the incentive to the non-compliance even though there may be lower equilibrium at **'L'** which is below the superior equilibrium at **'Z'**. Thus environmental degradation continues to grow and there is a problem in achieving sustainable development due to this free-rider problem of non-compliance.

Keeping the details of the diagram D, the free-rider gain is shown in the area of **QKY** and the loss to humanity is depicted in the area of **KDptLY**. In order to achieve the superior equilibrium and the compliance, the development expenditure incurred by the Third World nations has to be shared by the developed nations and this is the '*Empowerment of Sustainable Development*' as shown by the area **OKQ**, which results in achieving the Superior equilibrium at 2 as shows in the diagram F. The empowerment of Sustainable development achieves compliance with maximum participation of nations.

APPENDIX I

Convention on Desertification

UNITED NATIONS CONVENTION TO COMBAT DESERTIFICATION IN THOSE COUNTRIES EXPERIENCING SERIOUS DROUGHT AND/OR DESERTIFICATION, PARTICULARLY IN AFRICA

The Parties to this Convention,

Affirming that human beings in affected or threatened areas are at the centre of concerns to combat desertification and mitigate the effects of drought,

Reflecting the urgent concern of the international community, including States and international organizations, about the adverse impacts of desertification and drought,

Aware that arid, semi-arid and dry sub-humid areas together account for a significant proportion of the Earth's land area and are the habitat and source of livelihood for a large segment of its population,

Acknowledging that desertification and drought are problems of global dimension in that they affect all regions of the world and that joint action of the international community is needed to combat desertification and/or mitigate the effects of drought,

Noting the high concentration of developing countries, notably the least developed countries, among those experiencing serious drought/or desertification, and the particularly tragic consequences of these phenomena in Africa,

Noting also that desertification is caused by complex

interactions among physical, biological, political, social cultural and economic factors,

Considering the impact of trade and relevant aspects of international economic relations on the ability of affected countries to combat desertification adequately,

Conscious that sustainable economic growth, social development and poverty eradication are priorities of affected developing countries, particularly in Africa, and are essential to meeting sustainability objectives,

Mindful that desertification and drought affect sustainable development through their interrelationship with important social problems such as poverty, poor health and nutrition, lack of food security, and those arising from migration, displacement of persons and demographic dynamics,

Appreciating the significance of the past efforts and experience of States and international organizations in combating desertification and mitigating the effect of drought, particularly in implementing the Plan of Action to Combat Desertification which was adopted at the United Nations Conference on Desertification in 1977,

Realizing that despite efforts in the past, progress in combating desertification and mitigating the effects of drought has not met expectations and that a new and more effective approach is needed at all levels within the framework of sustainable development,

Recognizing the validity and relevance of decisions adopted at the United Nations Conference on Environment and Development, particularly of Agenda 21 and its chapter 12, which provide a basis for combating desertification,

Reaffirming in this light the commitments of developed countries as contained in paragraph 13 of chapter 33 of Agenda 21,

Recalling General Assembly resolution 47/188, particularly the priority in it prescribed for Africa, and all other relevant United Nations resolutions, decisions and programs on desertification and drought, as well as relevant declarations by African countries and those from other regions,

Reaffirming the Rio Declaration on Environment and Development which states, in its Principle 2, that States have, in accordance with the Charter of the United Nations and the principles of international law, the sovereign right to exploit their own resources pursuant to their own environmental and developmental policies, and the responsibility to ensure that activities within their jurisdiction or control do not cause damage to the environment of other States or of areas beyond the limits of national jurisdiction,

Recognizing that national Governments play a critical role in combating desertification and mitigating the effects of drought and that progress in that respect depends on local implementation of action programmes in affected areas,

Recognizing also the importance and necessity of international cooperation and partnership in combating desertification and mitigating the effects of drought,

Recognizing further the importance of the provision to affected developing countries, particularly in Africa, of effective means, *inter alia* substantial financial resources, including new and additional funding, and access to technology, without which it will be difficult for them to implement fully their commitments under this Convention,

Expressing concern over the impact of desertification and drought on affected countries in Central Asia and the Transcutaneous,

Stressing the important role played by women in regions affected by desertification and/or drought, particularly in rural areas of developing countries, and the importance of ensuring the full participation of both men and women at all levels in programmes to combat desertification and mitigate the effects of drought,

Emphasizing the special role of non-governmenta organizations and other major groups in programmes to combat desertification and mitigate the effects of drought,

Bearing in mind the relationship between desertification and other environmental problems of global dimension facing the international and national communities,

Bearing also in mind the contribution that combating desertification can make to achieving the objectives of the United Nations Framework Convention on Climate Change, the Convention on Biological Diversity and other related environmental conventions,

Believing that strategies to combat desertification and mitigate the effects of drought will be most effective if they are based on sound systematic observation and rigorous scientific knowledge and if they are continuously re-evaluated,

Recognizing the urgent need to improve the effectiveness and coordination of international cooperation to facilitate the implementation of national plans and priorities,

Determined to take appropriate action in combating desertification and mitigating the effects of drought for the benefit of present and future generations,

Have agreed *as follows:*

PART I: INTRODUCTION

Article 1. Use of Terms

For the purposes of this Convention:

(a) "Desertification" means land degradation in arid, semi-arid and dry sub-humid areas resulting from various factors, including climatic variations and human activities;

(b) "Combating desertification" includes activities which are part of the integrated development of land in arid, semi-arid and dry sub-humid areas for sustainable development which are aimed at:

(i) prevention and/or reduction of land degradation;

(ii) rehabilitation of partly degraded land; and

(iii) reclamation of decertified land;

(c) "drought" means the naturally occurring phenomenon that exists when precipitation has been significantly below normal recorded levels, causing serious hydrological imbalances that adversely affect land resource production systems;

(d) "mitigating the effects of drought" means activities related to the prediction of drought and intended to reduce the vulnerability of society and natural systems to drought as it relates to combating desertification;

(e) "land" means the terrestrial bio-productive system that comprises soil, vegetation, other biota, and the ecological and hydrological processes that operate within the system;

(f) "land degradation" means reduction or loss, in arid, semi-arid and dry sub-humid areas, of the biological or economic productivity and complexity of rainfed cropland, irrigated cropland, or range, pasture, forest and woodlands resulting from land uses or from a process or combination of processes, including processes arising from human activities and habitation patterns, such as:

  (i) soil erosion caused by wind and/or water;

  (ii) deterioration of the physical, chemical and biological or economic properties of soils; and

  (iii) long-term loss of natural vegetation;

(g) "arid, semi-arid and dry sub-humid areas" means areas, other than polar and sub-polar regions, in which the ratio of annual precipitation to potential evapotranspiration falls within the range from 0.05 to 0.65;

(h) "affected areas" means arid, semi-arid and/or dry sub-humid areas affected or threatened by desertification;

(i) "affected countries" means countries whose lands include, in whole or in part, affected areas;

(j) "regional economic integration organization" means an organization constituted by sovereign States of a given region which has competence in respect of matters governed by this Convention and has been duly authorized, in accordance with its internal procedures, to sign, ratify, accept, approve or accede to this Convention;

(k) "developed country Parties" means developed country Parties and regional economic integration organizations constituted by developed countries.

Article 2. Objective

1. The objective of this Convention is to combat desertification and mitigate the effects of drought in countries experiencing serious drought and/or desertification, particularly in Africa, through effective action at all levels, supported by international cooperation and partnership arrangements, in the framework of an integrated approach which is consistent with Agenda 21, with a view to contributing to the achievement of sustainable development in affected areas.
2. Achieving this objective will involve long-term integrated strategies that focus simultaneously, in affected areas, on improved productivity of land, and the rehabilitation, conservation and sustainable management of land and water resources, leading to improved living conditions, in particular at the community level.

Article 3. Principles

In order to achieve the objective of this Convention and to implement its provisions, the Parties shall be guided, *inter alia,* by the following:

(a) The Parties should ensure that decisions on the design and implementation of programmes to combat desertification and/or mitigate the effects of drought are taken with the participation of populations and local communities and that an enabling environment is created at higher levels to facilitate action at national and local levels;

(b) the Parties should, in a spirit of international solidarity and partnership, improve cooperation and coordination at subregional, regional and international levels, and better focus financial, human, organizational and technical resources where they are needed;

(c) the Parties should develop, in a spirit of partnership, cooperation among all levels of government, communities, non-governmental organizations and landholders to establish a better understanding of the nature and value of land and scarce water resources in affected areas and to work towards their sustainable use; and

(d) the Parties should take into full consideration the special needs and circumstances of affected developing country Parties, particularly the least developed among them.

PART II: GENERAL PROVISIONS

Article 4. General Obligations

1. The Parties shall implement their obligations under this Convention, individually or jointly, either through existing or prospective bilateral and multilateral arrangements or a combination thereof, as appropriate, emphasizing the need to coordinate efforts and develop a coherent long-term strategy at all levels.
2. In pursuing the objective of this Convention, the Parties shall:

   (a) adopt an integrated approach addressing the physical biological and socio-economic aspects of the processes of desertification and drought;

   (b) give due attention, within the relevant international and regional bodies, to the situation of affected developing country Parties with regard to international trade, marketing arrangements and debt with a view to establishing an enabling international environment conducive to the promotion of sustainable development;

(c) integrate strategies for poverty eradication into efforts to combat desertification and mitigate the effects of drought;

(d) promote cooperation among affected country Parties the fields of environmental protection and the conservation of land and water resources, as they relate to desertification and drought;

(e) strengthen subregional, regional and international cooperation;

(f) cooperate within relevant intergovernmental organizations;

(g) determine institutional mechanisms, if appropriate, keeping in mind the need to avoid duplication; and

(h) promote the use of existing bilateral and multilateral financial mechanisms and arrangements that mobilize and channel substantial financial resources of affected developing country Parties combating desertification and mitigating the effects of drought.

3. Affected developing country Parties are eligible for assistance in the implementation of the Convention.

Article 5. Obligations of Affected Country Parties

In addition to their obligations pursuant to article 4, affected country Parties undertake to:

(a) give due priority to combating desertification and mitigating the effects of drought, and allocate adequate resources in accordance with their circumstances and capabilities;

(b) establish strategies and priorities, within the framework of sustainable development plans and/or policies to combat desertification and mitigate the effects of drought;

(c) address the underlying causes of desertification and pay special attention to the socio-economic factors contributing to desertification processes;

(d) promote awareness and facilitate the participation of local populations, particularly women and youth, with the support of non-governmental organizations, in efforts to combat desertification and mitigate the effects of drought; and

(e) provide an enabling environment by strengthening, as appropriate, relevant existing legislation and, where they do not exist, enacting new laws and establishing long-term policies and action programmes.

Article 6. Obligations of Developed Country Parties

In addition to their general obligations pursuant to article 4, developed country Parties undertake to:

(a) actively support as agreed, individually or jointly, the efforts of affected developing country Parties, particularly those in Africa, and the least developed countries, to combat desertification and mitigate the effects of drought;

(b) provide substantial financial resources and other forms of support to assist affected developing country Parties, particularly those in Africa, effectively to develop and implement their own long-term plans and strategies to combat desertification and mitigate the effects of drought;

(c) promote the mobilization of new and additional funding pursuant to article 20, paragraph 2(b);

(d) encourage the mobilization of funding from the private sector and other non-governmental sources; and

(e) promote and facilitate access by affected country Parties, particularly affected developing country Parties, to appropriate technology, knowledge and know-how.

Article 7. Priority for Africa

In implementing thick Convention, the Parties shall give priority to affected African country Parties, in the light of the particular situation prevailing in that region, while not neglecting affected developing country Parties in other regions.

Article 8. Relationship with Other Conventions

1. The Parties shall encourage the coordination of activities carried out under this Convention and, if they are Parties to them, under other relevant international agreements, particularly the United Nations Framework Convention on Climate Change and the Convention on Biological Diversity, in order to derive maximum benefit from activities under each agreement while avoiding duplicationof effort. The Parties shall encourage the conduct of joint programmes, particularly in the fields of research, training, systematic observation and information collection and exchange, to the extent that such activities may contribute to achieving the objectives of the agreements concerned.
2. The provisions of this Convention shall not affect the rights and obligations of any Party deriving from a bilateral, regional or international agreement into which it has entered prior to the entry into force of this Convention for it.

PART III: ACTION PROGRAMMES, SCIENTIFIC AND TECHNICAL COOPERATION AND SUPPORTING MEASURES

SECTION 1: *Action Programmes*

Article 9. Basic Approach

1. In carrying out their obligations pursuant to article 5, affected developing country Parties and any other affected country Party in the framework of its regional implementation annex or, otherwise, that has notified the

Permanent Secretariat in writing of its intention to prepare a national action programme, shall, as appropriate, prepare, make public and implement national action programmes, utilizing and building, to the extent possible, on existing relevant successful plans and programmes, and subregional and regional action programmes, as the central element of the strategy to combat desertification and mitigate the effects of drought. Such programmes shall be updated through a continuing participatory process on the basis of lessons from field action, as well as the results of research. The preparation of national action programmes shall be closely interlinked with other efforts to formulate national policies for sustainable development.

2. In the provision by developed country Parties of different forms of assistance under the terms of article 6, priority shall be given to supporting, as agreed, a national, subregional and regional action programmes of affected developing country Parties, particularly those in Africa, either directly or through relevant multilateral organizations or both.
3. The Parties shall encourage organs, funds and programmes of the United Nations system and other relevant intergovernmental organizations, academic institutions, the scientific community and non-governmental organizations in a position to cooperate, in accordance with their mandates and capabilities, to support the elaboration, implementation and follow-up of action programmes.

Article 10. National Action Programmes

1. The purpose of national action programmes is to identify the factors contributing to desertification and practical measures necessary to combat desertification and mitigate the effects of drought.
2. National action programmes shall specify the respective roles of government, local communities and land users

and the resources available and needed. They shall, *inter alia:*

(a) incorporate long-term strategies to combat desertification and mitigate the effects of drought, emphasize implementation and be integrated with national policies for sustainable development;

(b) allow for modifications to be made in response to changing circumstances and be sufficiently flexible at the local level to cope with different socio-economic, biological and geo-physical conditions;

(c) give particular attention to the implementation of preventive measures for lands that are not yet degraded or which are only slightly degraded;

(d) enhance national climatological, meteorological and hydrological capabilities and the means to provide for drought early warning;

(e) promote policies and strengthen institutional frameworks which develop cooperation and coordination, in a spirit of partnership, between the donor community, governments at all levels, local populations and community groups, and facilitate access by local populations to appropriate information and technology;

(f) provide for effective participation at the local, national and regional levels of non-governmental organizations and local populations, both women and men, particularly resource users, including farmers and pastoralists and their representative organizations, in policy planning, decision-making and implementation and review of national action programmes; and

(g) require regular review of, and progress reports on, their implementation.

3. National action programmes may include, *inter alia,* some or all of the following measures to prepare for and mitigate the effects of drought:

(a) establishment and/or strengthening, as appropriate, of early warning systems, including local and national facilities and joint systems at the subregional and regional levels, and mechanisms for assisting environmentally displaced persons;

(b) strengthening of drought preparedness and management, including drought contingency plans at the local, national, subregional and regional levels, which take into consideration seasonal to interannual climate predictions;

(c) establishment and/or strengthening, as appropriate, of food security systems, including storage and marketing facilities, particularly in rural areas;

(d) establishment of alternative livelihood projects that could provide incomes in drought prone areas; and

(e) development of sustainable irrigation programmes for both crops and livestock.

4. Taking into account the circumstances and requirements specific to each affected country Party, national action programmes include, as appropriate, *inter alia,* measures in some or all of the following priority fields as they relate to combating desertification and mitigating the effects of drought in affected areas and to their populations: promotion of alternative livelihoods and improvement of national economic environments with a view to strengthening programmes aimed at the eradication of poverty and at ensuring food security; demographic dynamics; sustainable management of natural resources; sustainable agricultural practices; development and efficient use of various energy sources; institutional and legal frameworks; strengthening of capabilities for assessment and systematic observation, including hydrological and meteorological services, and capacity building, education and public awareness.

Article 11. Subregional and Regional Action Programmes

Affected country Parties shall consult and cooperate to prepare, as appropriate, in accordance with relevant regional implementation annexes, subregional and/or regional action programmes to harmonize, complement and increase the efficiency of national programmes. The provisions of article 10 shall apply *mutatis mutandis* to subregional and regional programmes. Such cooperation may include agreed joint programmes for the sustainable management of transboundary natural resources, scientific and technical cooperation, and strengthening of relevant institutions.

Article 12. International Cooperation

Affected country Parties, in collaboration with other Parties and the international community, should cooperate to ensure the promotion of an enabling international environment in the implementation of the Convention. Such cooperation should also cover fields of technology transfer as well as scientific research and development, information collection and dissemination and financial resources.

Article 13. Support for the Elaboration and Implementation of Action Programmes

1. Measures to support action programmes pursuant to article 9 include, *inter alia:*
   (a) financial cooperation to provide predictability for action programmes, allowing for necessary long-term planning;
   (b) elaboration and use of cooperation mechanisms which better enable support at the local level; and
   (c) as appropriate, administrative and budgetary procedures that increase the efficiency of cooperation and of support programmes.
2. In providing such support to affected developing country Parties, priority shall be given to African country Parties and to least developed country Parties.

Article 14. Coordination in the Elaboration and Implementation of Action Programmes

1. The Parties shall work closely together, directly and through relevant intergovernmental organizations, in the elaboration and implementation of action programmes.
2. The Parties shall develop operational mechanisms, particularly at the national and field levels, to ensure the fullest possible coordination among developed country Parties, developing country Parties and relevant intergovernmental and non-governmental organizations, in order to avoid duplication, harmonize interventions and approaches, and maximize the impact of assistance. In affected developing country Parties, priority will be given to coordinating activities related to international cooperation in order to maximize the efficient use of resources, to ensure responsive assistance, and to facilitate the implementation of national action programmes and priorities under this Convention.

Article 15. Regional Implementation Annexes

Elements for incorporation in action programmes shall be selected and adapted to the socio-economic, geographical and climate factors applicable to affected country Parties or regions, as well as to their level of development. Guidelines for the preparation of action programmes and their exact focus and content for particular subregions are set out in the regional implementation annexes.

SECTION 2: *Scientific and Technical Cooperation*

Article 16: Information Collection, Analysis and Exchange

The Parties agree, according to their respective capabilities, to integrate and coordinate the collection, analysis and exchange of relevant short term and long term data information to ensure systematic observation of land degradation in affected areas and to understand better and assess the processes and effects of drought and desertification. This would help accomplish, *inter alia,* early warning and advance planning for periods of adverse climatic variation in a form suited for practical application by users at all levels, including especially local populations. To this end, they shall, as appropriate:

(a) Facilitate and strengthen the functioning of the global network of institutions and facilities for the collection, analysis and exchange of information, as well as for systematic observation at all levels, which shall, *inter alia:*

  (i) aim to use relevant modern technology for data collection, transmission and assessment on land degradation; and

  (ii) encompass relevant data and stations, including in remote areas;

  (iii) use and disseminate modern technology for data collection, transmission and assessment on land degradation; and

  (iv) link national, subregional and regional data and information centres more closely with global information sources;

(b) ensure that the collection, analysis and exchange of information address the needs of local communities and those of decision makers, with a view to resolving specific problems, and that local communities are involved in these activities;

(c) support and further develop bilateral and multilateral programmes and projects aimed at defining, conducting, assessing and financing the collection, analysis and exchange of data and information, including, *inter alia,* integrated sets of physical, biological, social and economic indicators;

(d) make full use of the expertise of competent intergovernmental and non-governmental organizations, particularly to disseminate relevant information and experiences among target groups in different regions;

(e) give full weight to the collection, analysis and exchange of socio-economic data, and their integration with physical and biological data;

(f) exchange and make fully, openly and promptly available information from all publicly available sources relevant to combating desertification and mitigating the effects of drought; and

(g) subject to their respective national legislation and/or policies, exchange information on local and traditional knowledge, ensuring adequate protection for it and providing appropriate return from the benefits derived from it, on an equitable basis and on mutually agreed terms, to the local populations concerned.

Article 17. Research and Development

1. The parties undertake, according to their respective capabilities, to promote technical and scientific cooperation in the fields of combating desertification and mitigating the effects of drought through appropriate national, subregional, regional and international institutions. To this end, they shall support research activities that:

   (a) Contribute to increased knowledge of the processes leading to desertification and drought and the impact of, and distinction between, causal factors, both natural and human, with a view to combating, and achieving improved productivity as well as sustainable use and management of resources;

   (b) respond to well defined objectives, address the specific needs of local populations and lead to the identification and implementation of solutions that improve the living standards of people in affected areas;

   (c) protect, integrate, enhance and validate traditional and local knowledge, know-how and practices, ensuring, subject to their respective national legislation and/or policies, that the owners of that knowledge will directly benefit on an equitable basis and on mutually agreed terms from any commercial utilization of it or from any technologically development derived from that knowledge;

(d) develop and strengthen national, subregional and regional research capabilities in affected developing country. Parties, particularly in Africa, including the development of local skills and the strengthening of appropriate capacities, especially in countries with a weak research base, giving particular attention to multidisciplinary and participative socio-economic research:

(e) take into account, where relevant, the relationship between poverty, migration caused by environmental factors, and desertification;

(f) promote the conduct of joint research programmes between national, subregional, regional and international research organizations, in both the public and private sectors, for the development of improved, affordable and accessible technologies for sustainable development through effective participation of local populations and communities; and

(g) enhance the availability of water resources in affected areas, by means, of, *inter alia,* cloud-seeding.

2. Research priorities for particular regions and subregions, reflecting different local conditions, should be included in action programmes. The Conference of the Parties shall review research priorities periodically on the advice of the Committee on Science and Technology.

Article 18. Transfer, Acquisition, Adaptation and Development of Technology

1. The Parties undertake, as mutually agreed and in

accordance with their respective national legislation and/or policies, to promote, finance and/or facilitate the financing of the transfer, acquisition, adaptation and development of environmentally sound, economically viable and socially acceptable technologies to the achievement of sustainable development in affected areas. Such cooperation shall be conducted bilaterally or multilaterally, as appropriate, making full use of the expertise of intergovernmental and non-governmental organizations. The Parties shall, in particular:

(a) Fully utilize relevant existing national, subregional, regional and international information systems and clearing houses for the dissemination of information on available technologies, their sources, their environmental risks and the broad terms under which they may be acquired;

(b) facilitate access, in particular by affected developing country Parties, on favourable terms, including on concessional and preferential terms, as mutually agreed, taking into account the need to protect intellectual property rights, to technologies most suitable to practical application for specific needs of local populations, paying special attention to the social, cultural, economic and environmental impact of such technology;

(c) facilitate technology cooperation among affected country Parties through financial assistance or other appropriate means;

(d) extend technology cooperation with affected developing country Parties, including, where relevant, joint ventures, especially to sectors which foster alternative livelihoods; and

(e) take appropriate measures to create domestic market conditions and incentives, fiscal or otherwise, conducive to the development, transfer, acquisition and adaptation of suitable technology, knowledge, know-how and practise, including measures to ensure adequate and effective protection of intellectual property rights.

2. The Parties shall, according to their respective capabilities, and subject to their respective national legislation and/or policies, protect, promote and use in particular relevant traditional and local technology, knowledge, know-how and practices and, to that end, they undertake to:
   (a) make inventories of such technology, knowledge, know-how and practices and potential uses with the participation of local populations, and disseminate such information, where appropriate, in cooperation with relevant intergovernmental and non-governmental organizations;
   (b) ensure that such technology, knowledge, know-how and practices are adequately protected and that local populations benefit directly, on an equitable basis and as mutually agreed, from any commercial utilization of them or from any technological development derived therefrom;
   (c) encourage and actively support the improvement and dissemination of such technology, knowledge, know-how and practices or of the development of new technology based on them; and
   (d) facilitate, as appropriate, the adaptation of such technology, knowledge, know-how and practices to wide use and integrate them with modern technology, as appropriate.

SECTION 3: *Supporting Measures*

Article 19. Capacity Building, Education and Public Awareness

1. The Parties recognize the significance of capacity building—that is to say, institution building, training and

development of relevant local and national capacities—in efforts to combat desertification and mitigate the effects of drought. They shall promote, as appropriate, capacity building:

(a) through the full participation at all levels of local people, particularly at the local level, especially women and youth, with the cooperation of non-governmental and local organizations;
(b) by strengthening training and research capacity at the national level in the field of desertification and drought;
(c) by establishing and/or strengthening support and extension services to disseminate relevant technology methods and techniques more effectively, and by training field agents and members of rural organizations in participatory approaches for the conservation and sustainable use of natural resources;
(d) by fostering the use and dissemination of the knowledge, know-how and practices of local people in technical cooperation programmes, wherever possible;
(e) by adapting, where necessary, relevant environmentally sound technology and traditional methods of agriculture and pastoralism to modern socio-economic conditions;
(f) by providing appropriate training and technology in the use of alternative energy sources, particularly renewable energy resources, aimed particularly at reducing dependence on wood for fuel;
(g) through cooperation, as mutually agreed, to strengthen the capacity of affected developing country Parties to develop and implement programmes in the field of collection, analysis and exchange of information pursuant to article 16;
(h) through innovative ways of promoting alternative livelihoods, including training in new skills;
(i) by training of decision makers, managers, and personnel who are responsible for the collection and analysis of

data for the dissemination and use of early warning information on drought conditions and for food production;

(j) through more effective operation of existing national institutions and legal frameworks and, where necessary, creation of new ones, along with strengthening of strategic planning and management; and

(k) by means of exchange visitor programmes to enhance capacity building in affected country Parties through a long-term, interactive process of alarming and study.

2. Affected developing country Parties shall conduct, in co-operation with other Parties and competent inter-governmental and non-governmental organizations, as appropriate, an interdisciplinary review of available capacity and facilities at the local and national levels, and the potential for strengthening them.

3. The Parties shall cooperate with each other and through competent intergovernmental organizations, as well as with non-governmental organizations, in undertaking and supporting public awareness and educational programmes in both affected and, where relevant, unaffected country Parties to promote understanding of the causes and effects of desertification and drought and of the importance of meeting the objective of this Convention. To that end, they shall:

(a) organize awareness campaigns for the general public;

(b) promote, on a permanent basis, access by the public to relevant information, and wide public participation in education and awareness activities;

(c) encourage the establishment of associations that contribute to public awareness;

(d) develop and exchange educational and public awareness material, where possible in local languages, exchange and second experts to train personnel of affected developing country Parties in carrying out relevant education and awareness programmes, and fully utilize relevant educational material available in competent international bodies;

(e) assess educational needs in affected areas, elaborate appropriate school curricula and expand, as needed, educational and adult literacy for girls and women, on the identification, conservation and sustainable use and management of the natural resources of affected, areas; and

(f) develop interdisciplinary participatory programmes integrating desertification and drought awareness into educational systems and in non-formal, adult, distance and practical educational programmes.

4. The Conference of the Parties shall establish and/or strengthen networks of regional education and training centres to combat desertification and mitigate the effects of drought. These networks shall be coordinated by an institution created or designated for that purpose, in order to train scientific, technical and management personnel and to strengthen existing institutions responsible for education and training in affected country Parties, where appropriate, with a view to harmonizing programmes and to organizing exchanges of experience among them. These networks shall cooperate closely with relevant intergovernmental and non-governmental organizations to avoid duplication of effort.

Article 20. Financial Resources

1. Given the central importance of financing to the achievement of the objective of the Convention, the Parties, taking into account their capabilities, shall make every effort to ensure that adequate financial resources are available for programmes to combat desertification and mitigate the effects of drought.
2. In this connection developed country Parties, while giving priority to affected African country Parties without

neglecting affected developing country Parties in other regions, in accordance with article 7 undertake to:

(a) mobilize substantial financial resources, including grants and concessional loans, in order to support the implementation of programmes to combat desertification and mitigate the effects of drought;

(b) promote the mobilization of adequate, timely and predictable financial resources, including new and additional funding from the Global Environment Facility of the agreed incremental costs of those activities concerning desertification that relate to its four focal areas, in conformity with the relevant provisions of the Instrument establishing the Global Environment Facility;

(c) facilitate through international cooperation the transfer of technology, knowledge and know-how; and

(d) explore, in cooperation with affected developing country Parties, innovative methods and incentives for mobilizing and channelling resources, including those of foundations, non-governmental organizations and other private sector entities, particularly debt swaps and other innovative means which increase financing by reducing the external debt burden of affected developing country Parties, particularly those in Africa.

3. Affected developing country Parties, taking into account their capabilities, undertake to mobilize adequate financial resources for the implementation of their national action programmes.

4. In mobilizing financial resources the Parties shall seek full use and continued qualitative improvement of all national, bilateral and multilateral funding sources and mechanisms, using consortia, joint programmes and parallel financing, and shall seek to involve private sector funding sources and mechanisms, including those of non-governmental organizations. To this end, the Parties shall fully utilize the operational mechanisms developed pursuant to article 14.

5. In order to mobilize the financial resources necessary for affected developing country Parties to combat desertification and mitigate the effects of drought, the Parties shall:
   (a) rationalize and strengthen the management of resources already allocated for combating desertification and mitigating the effects of drought by using them more effectively and efficiently, assessing their successes and shortcomings, removing hindrances to their effective use and, where necessary, reorienting programmes in light of the integrated long-term approach adopted pursuant to this Convention;
   (b) give due priority and attention within the governing bodies of multilateral financial institutions, facilities and funds, including regional development banks and funds, to supporting affected developing country Parties, particularly those in Africa, in activities which advance implementation of the Convention notably action programmes they undertake in the framework of regional implementation annexes; and
   (c) examine ways in which regional and subregional cooperation can be strengthened to support efforts undertaken at the national level.
6. Other Parties are encouraged to provide, on a voluntary basis, knowledge, know-how and techniques related to desertification and/or financial resources to affected developing country Parties.
7. The full implementation by affected developing country Parties, particularly those in Africa, of their obligations under the Convention will be greatly assisted by the fulfillment by the developed country Parties of their obligations under the Convention, including in particular those regarding financial resources and transfer of technology. In fulfilling their obligations, developed country Parties should take fully into account that economic and

social development and poverty eradication are the first priorities of affected developing country Parties particularly those in Africa.

Article 21. Financial Mechanisms

1. The Conference of the Parties shall promote the availability of financial mechanisms and shall encourage such mechanisms to seek to maximize the availability of funding for affected developing country Parties, particularly those in Africa, to implement the Convention. To this end, the Conference of the Parties shall consider the adoption *inter alia* approaches and policies that:
   (a) facilitate the provision of necessary funding at the national, subregional, regional and global levels for activities pursuant to relevant provisions of the Conventions;
   (b) promote multiple-source funding approaches, mechanisms and arrangements and their assessment, consistent with article 20;
   (c) provide on a regular basis, to interested Parties and relevant intergovernmental and non-governmental organizations, information on available sources of funds and on funding patterns in order to facilitate coordination among them;
   (d) facilitate the establishment, as appropriate, of mechanisms, such as national desertification funds, including those involving the participation of non-governmental organizations, to channel financial resources rapidly and efficiently to the local level in affected developing country Parties; and
   (e) strengthen existing funds and financial mechanisms at the subregional levels, particularly in Africa, to support more effectively the implementation of the Convention.
2. The Conference of the Parties shall also encourage the provision, through various mechanisms within the United

Nations system and through multilateral financial institutions, of support at the national, subregional and regional levels to activities that enable developing country Parties to meet their obligation under the Convention.

3. Affected developing country Parties shall utilize, and where necessary, establish and/or strengthen, national coordinating mechanisms, integrated in national development programmes, that would ensure the efficient use of all available financial resources. They shall also utilize participatory processes involving non-governmental organizations, local group and the private sector, in raising funds, in elaborating as well as implementing programmes and in assuring access to funding by groups at the local level. These actions can be enhanced by improved coordination and flexible programming on the part of those providing assistance.
4. In order to increase the effectiveness and efficiency of existing financial mechanisms, a Global Mechanism to promote actions leading to the mobilization and channelling of substantial financial resources, including for the transfer of technology, on a grant basis, and/or on concessional or other terms, to affected developing country Parties, is hereby established. This Global Mechanism shall function under the authority and guidance of the Conference of the Parties and be accountable to it.
5. The Conference of the Parties shall identify, at its first ordinary session, an organization to house the Global Mechanism. The Conference of the Parties and the organization it has identified shall agree upon modalities for this Global Mechanism to ensure *inter alia* that such Mechanism:
   (a) identifies and draws up an inventory of relevant bilateral and multilateral cooperation programmes that are available to implement the Convention;
   (b) provides advice, on request, to Parties on innovative

methods of financing and sources of financial assistance and on improving the coordinating of cooperation activities at the national level;

(c) provides interested Parties and relevant inter-governmental and non-governmental organizations with information on available sources of funds and on funding patterns in order to facilitate coordination among them; and

(d) reports to the Conference of the Parties, beginning at its second ordinary session, on its activities.

6. The Conference of the Parties shall, at its first session, make appropriate arrangements with the organization it has identified to house the Global Mechanism for the administrative operation of such Mechanism, drawing to the extent possible on existing budgetary and human resources.

7. The Conference of the Parties shall, at its third ordinary session, review the policies, operational modalities and activities of the Global Mechanism accountable to it pursuant to paragraph 4, taking into account the provision of article 7. On the basis of this reviews, it shall consider and take appropriate action.

PART IV: INSTITUTIONS

Article 22. Conference of the Parties

1. A Conference of the Parties is hereby established.
2. The Conference of the Parties is the supreme body of the Convention. It shall make, within its mandate, the decisions necessary to promote its effective implementation. In particular, it shall:

(a) regularly review the implementation of Convention and the functioning of its institutional arrangements in the light of the experience gained at the national, subregional, regional and international levels and on the basis of the evolution of scientific and technological knowledge;

(b) promote and facilitate the exchange of information on measures adopted by the Parties, and determine the form and timetable for transmitting the information to be submitted pursuant to article 26, review the reports and make recommendations on them;

(c) establish such subsidiary bodies as are deemed necessary for the implementation of the Convention;

(d) review reports submitted by its subsidiary bodies and provide guidance to them;

(e) agree upon and adopt, by consensus, rules of procedure and financial rules for itself and any subsidiary bodies;

(f) adopt amendments to the Convention pursuant to article 30 and 31;

(g) approve a programme and budget for its activities, including those of its subsidiary bodies, and undertake necessary arrangements for their financing;

(h) as appropriate, seek the cooperation of, and utilize the services of and information provided by, competent bodies or agencies, whether national or international, intergovernmental or non-governmental;

(i) promote and strengthen the relationship with other relevant conventions while avoiding duplication of effort; and

(j) exercise such other functions as may be necessary for the achievement of the objective of the Convention.

3. The Conference of the Parties shall, at its first session, adopt its own rules of procedure, by consensus, which shall include decision-making procedures for matters not already covered by decision-making procedures stipulated in the Convention. Such procedures may include specified majorities required for the adoption of particular decisions.

4. The first session of the Conference of the Parties shall be convened by the interim secretariat refereed to in article 35

and shall take place not later than one year after the date of entry into force of the Convention. Unless otherwise decided by the Conference of the Parties, the second, third and fourth ordinary sessions shall be held yearly, and thereafter, ordinary sessions shall be held every two years.

5. Extraordinary sessions of the Conference of the Parties shall be held at such other times as may be decided either by the Conference of the parties in ordinary session or at the written request of any party, provided that, within three months of the request communicated to the Parties by the Permanent Secretariat, it is supported by at least one third of the Parties.
6. At each ordinary session, the Conference of the Parties shall elect a Bureau. The structure and functions of the Bureau shall be determined in the rules of procedure. In appointing the Bureau, due regard shall be paid to the need to ensure equitable geographical distribution and adequate representation of affected country Parties, particularly those in Africa.
7. The United Nations, its specialized agencies and any State member thereof or observers thereto not Party to the Convention, may be represented at sessions of the Conference of the Parties as observers. Any body or agency, whether national or international, governmental or non-governmental, which is qualified on matters covered by the Convention, and which has informed the Permanent Secretariat of its wish to be represented at a session of the Conference of the Parties as an observer, may be so admitted unless at least one third of the Parties present object. The admission and participation of observers shall be subject to the rules of procedure adopted by the Conference of the Parties.
8. The Conference of the Parties may request competent national and international organizations which have relevant expertise to provide it with information relevant to

article 16, paragraph (g), article 17, paragraph I (c) and article 18, paragraph 2(b).

Article 23. Permanent Secretariat

1. A Permanent Secretariat is hereby established.
2. The functions of the Permanent Secretariat shall be:
   (a) to make arrangements for sessions of the Conference of the Parties and its subsidiary bodies established under the Convention and to provide them with services as required;
   (b) to complete and transmit reports submitted to it;
   (c) to facilitate assistance to affected developing country Parties, on request, particularly those in Africa, in the compilation and communication for information required under the Convention;
   (d) to coordinate its activities with the secretariats of other relevant international bodies and conventions;
   (e) to enter, under the guidance of the Conference of the Parties, into such administrative and contractual arrangements as may be required for the effective discharge of its functions;
   (f) to prepare reports on the execution of its functions under this Convention and present them to the Conference of the Parties; and
   (g) to perform such other secretariat functions as may be determined by the Conference of the Parties.
3. The Conference of the Parties, at its first session, shal designate a Permanent Secretariat and make arrangements for its functioning.

Article 24. Committee on Science and Technology

1. A Committee on Science and Technology is hereby established as a subsidiary body of the Conference of the Parties to provide it with information and advice on scientific and technological matters relating to combating

desertifications and mitigating the effects of drought. The Committee shall meet in conjunction with the ordinary session of the Conference of the Parties and shall be multidisciplinary and open to the participation of all Parties. It shall be composed of government representatives competent in the relevant fields of expertise. The Conference of the Parties shall decide, at its first session, the terms of reference of the Committee.

2. The Conference of the Parties shall establish and maintain a roster of independent experts with expertise and experience in the relevant fields. The roster shall be based on nominations received in writing from the Parties, taking into account the need for a multidisciplinary approach and broad geographical representation.
3. The Conference of the Parties may, as necessary, appoint ad hoc panels to provide it, through the Committee, with information and advice on specific issues regarding the state of the art in fields of science and technology relevant to combating desertification and mitigating the effects of drought. These panels shall be composed of experts whose names are taken from the roster, taking into account the need for a multidisciplinary approach and broad geographical representation. These experts shall have scientific backgrounds and field experience and shall be appointed by the Conference of the Parties on the recommendation of the Committee. The Conference of the Parties shall decide on the terms of reference and the modalities of work of these panels.

Article 25. Networking of Institutions, Agencies and Bodies

1. The Committee on Science and Technology shall, under the supervision of the Conference of the Parties, make provision for the undertaking of a survey and evaluation of the relevant existing networking institutions, agencies and

bodies willing to become units of a network. Such a network shall support the implementation of the Convention.

2. On the basis of the results of the survey and evaluation referred to in paragraph 1, the Committee on Science and Technology shall make recommendations to the Conference of the Parties on ways and means to facilitate and strengthen networking of the units at the local, national and other levels, with a view to ensuring that the thematic needs set out in articles 16 to 19 are addressed.
3. Taking into account these recommendation, the Conference of the Parties shall :
   (a) identify those national, subregional, regional and international units that are most appropriate for networking, and recommend operational procedures, and a time frame for them; and
   (b) identify the units best suited to facilitating and strengthening such networking at all levels.

PART V: PROCEDURES

Article 26. Communication of Information

1. Each Party shall communicate to the Conference of the Parties for consideration at its ordinary sessions, through the Permanent Secretariat, reports on the measures which it has taken for the implementation of the Convention. The Conference of the Parties shall determine the timetable for submission and the format of such reports.
2. Affected country Parties shall provide a description of the strategies established pursuant to Article 5 and of any relevant information on their implementation.
3. Affected country Parties which implement action programmes pursuant to Articles 9 to 15 shall provide a detailed description of the programmes and of their implementation.

4. Any group of affected country Parties may make a joint communication on measures taken at the subregional and/or regional levels in the framework of action programmes.
5. Developed country Parties shall report on measures taken to assist in the preparation and implementation of action programmes, including information on the financial resources they have provided, or are providing, under the Convention.
6. Information communicated pursuant to paragraphs 1 to 4 shall be transmitted by the Permanent Secretariat as soon as possible to the Conference of the Parties and to any relevant subsidiary body.
7. The Conference of the Parties shall facilitate the provision to affected developing countries, particularly those in Africa, on request, of technical and financial support in compiling and communicating information in accordance with this article, as well as identifying the technical and financial needs associated with action programmes.

Article 27. Measures to Resolve Questions on Implementation

The Conference of the Parties shall consider and adopt procedure and institutional mechanisms for the resolution of questions that may arise with regard to the implementation of the Convention.

Article 28. Settlement of Disputes

1. Parties shall settle any dispute between them concerning the interpretation or application of the Convention through negotiation or other peaceful means of their own choice.
2. When ratifying, accepting, approving, or acceding to the Convention, or at any time thereafter, a Party which is not a regional economic integration organization may declare

in a written instrument submitted to the Depositary that, in respect of any dispute concerning the interpretation or application of the Convention, it recognizes one or both of the following means of dispute settlement as compulsory in relation to any Party accepting the same obligation :

(a) arbitration in accordance with procedures adopted by the Conference of the Parties in an annex as soon as practicable;

(b) submission of the dispute to the International Court of Justice.

3. A Party which is a regional economic integration organization may make a declaration with like effect in relation to arbitration in accordance with the procedure referred to in paragraph 2(a).
4. A declaration made pursuant to paragraph 2 shall remain in force until it expires in accordance with its terms or until three months after written notice of its revocation has been deposited with the Depositary.
5. The expiry of a declaration, a notice of revocation or a new declaration shall not in any way affect proceedings pending before an arbitral tribunal or the International Court of Justice unless the Parties to the dispute otherwise agree.
6. If the Parties to a dispute have not accepted the same or any procedure pursuant to paragraph 2 and if they have not been able to settle their dispute within twelve months following notification by one Party to another that a dispute exists between them, the dispute shall be submitted to conciliation at the request of any Party to the dispute, in accordance with procedures adopted by the Conference of the Parties in an annex as soon as practicable.

Article 29. Status of Annexes

1. Annexes form an integral part of the Convention and, unless expressly provided otherwise, a reference to the

Convention also constitutes a reference to its annexes.
2. The Parties shall interpret the provisions of the annexes in a manner that is in conformity with their rights and obligations under the articles of this Convention.

Article 30. Amendments to the Convention

1. Any Party may propose amendments to the Convention.
2. Amendments to the Convention shall be adopted at an ordinary session of the Conference of the Parties. The text of any proposed amendment shall be communicated to the Parties by the Permanent Secretariat at least six months before the meeting at which it is proposed for adoption. The Permanent Secretariat shall also communicate proposed amendments to the signatories to the Convention.
3. The Parties shall make every effort to reach agreement on any proposed amendment to the Convention by consensus. If all efforts at consensus have been exhausted and no agreement is reached, the amendment shall, as a last resort, be adopted by a two-thirds majority vote of the Parties present and voting at the meeting. The adopted amendment shall be communicated by the Permanent Secretariat to the Depositary, who shall circulate it to all Parties for their ratification, acceptance, approval or accession.
4. Instruments of ratification, acceptance, approval or accession in respect of an amendment shall be deposited with the Depositary. An amendment adopted pursuant to paragraph 3 shall enter into force for those Parties having accepted it on the ninetieth day after the date of receipt by the Depositary of an instrument of ratification, acceptance, approval or accession by at least two-thirds of the Parties to the Convention which were Parties at the time of the adoption of the amendment.
5. The amendment shall enter into force for any other Party on the ninetieth day after the date on which that Party deposits with the Depositary its instrument of ratification,

acceptance or approval of, or accession to the said amendment.

6. For the purposes of this Article and Article 31, "Parties present and voting" means Parties present and casting an affirmative or negative vote.

Article 31. Adoption and Amendment of Annexes

1. Any additional annex to the Convention and any amendment to an annex shall be proposed and adopted in accordance with the procedure for amendment of the Convention set forth in Article 30, provided that, in adopting an additional regional implementation annex or amendment to any regional implementation annex, the majority provided for in that article shall include a two-thirds majority vote of the Parties of the region concerned present and voting. The adoption or amendment of an annex shall be communicated by the Depositary to all Parties.
2. An annex, other than an additional regional implementation annex, or an amendment to an annex, other than an amendment to any regional implementation annex, that has been adopted in accordance with paragraph 1, shall enter into force for all Parties to the Convention six months after the date of communication by the Depositary to such Parties of the adoption of such annex or amendment, except for those Parties that have notified the Depositary in writing within that period of their non-acceptance of such annex or amendment. Such annex or amendment shall enter into force for Parties which withdraw their notification of non-acceptance on the ninetieth day after the date on which withdrawal of such notification has been received by the Depositary.
3. An additional regional implementation annex or amendment to any regional implementation annex that has been adopted in accordance with paragraph 1, shall enter

into force for all Parties to the Convention six months after the date of the communication by the Depositary to such Parties of the adoption of such annex or amendment, except with respect to:

(a) any Party that has notified the Depositary in writing, within such six month period, of its non acceptance of that additional regional implementation annex or of the amendment to the regional implementation annex, in which case such annex or amendment shall enter into force for Parties which withdraw their notification of non acceptance on the ninetieth day after the date on which withdrawal of such notification has been received by the Depositary; and

(b) any Party that has made a declaration with respect to additional regional implementation annexes or amendments to regional implementation annexes in accordance with Article 34, paragraph 4, in which case any such annex or amendment shall enter into force for such a Party on the ninetieth day after the date of deposit with the Depositary of its instrument of ratification, acceptance, approval or accession with respect to such annex or amendment.

4. If the adoption of an annex or an amendment to an annex involves an amendment to the Convention, that annex or amendment to an annex shall not enter into force until such time as the amendment to the Convention enters into force.

Article 32. Right to Vote

1. Except as provided for in paragraph 2, each Party to the Convention shall have one vote.
2. Regional economic integration organizations, in matters within their competence, shall exercise their right to vote with a number of votes equal to the number of their member States that are Parties to the Convention. Such an

organization shall not exercise its right to vote if any of its member States exercises its right, and vice versa.

PART VI: FINAL PROVISIONS

Article 33. Signature

This Convention shall be opened for signature at Paris, on 14, 15 October 1994, by States Members of the United Nations or any of its specialized agencies or that are Parties to the Statute of the International Court of Justice and by regional economic integration organizations. It shall remain open for signature, thereafter, at the United Nations Headquarters in New York until 13 October, 1995.

Article 34. Ratification, Acceptance, Approval and Accession

1. The Convention shall be subject to ratification, acceptance, approval or accession by States and by regional economic integration organizations. It shall be open for accession from the day after the date on which the Convention is closed for signature. Instruments of ratification, acceptance, approval or accession shall be deposited with the Depositary.
2. Any regional economic integration organization which becomes a Party to the Convention without any of its member States being a Party to the Convention shall be bound by all the obligations under the Convention. Where one or more member States of such an organization are also Party to the Convention, the organization and its member States shall decide on their respective responsibilities for the performance of their obligations under the Convention. In such cases, the organization and the member States shall not be entitled to exercise rights under the Convention concurrently.
3. In their instruments of ratification, acceptance, approval or

accession, regional economic integration organizations shall declare the extent of their competence with respect to the matters governed by the Convention. They shall also promptly inform the Depositary, who shall in turn inform the Parties, of any substantial modification in the extent of their competence.

4. In its instrument of ratification, acceptance, approval or accession, any Party may declare that, with respect to it, any additional regional implementation annex or any amendment to any regional implementation annex shall enter into force only upon the deposit of its instrument of ratification, acceptance, approval or accession with respect thereto.

Article 35. Interim Arrangements

The secretariat functions referred to in Article 23 will be carried out on an interim basis by the secretariat established by the General Assembly of the United Nations in its resolution 47/188 of 22 December, 1992, until the completion of the first session of the Conference of the Parties.

Article 36. Entry into Force

1. The Convention shall enter into force on the ninetieth day after the date of deposit of the fiftieth instrument of ratification, acceptance, approval or accession.
2. For each State or regional economic integration organization ratifying, accepting, approving or acceding to the Convention after the deposit of the fiftieth instrument of ratification, acceptance, approval or accession, the Convention shall enter into force on the ninetieth day after the date of deposit by such State or regional economic integration organization of its instrument of ratification, acceptance, approval or accession.
3. For the purposes of paragraphs 1 and 2, any instrument deposited by a regional economic integration organization

shall not be counted as additional to those deposited by States members of the organization.

Article 37. Reservations

No reservations may be made to this Convention.

Article 38. Withdrawal

1. At any time after three years from the date on which the Convention has entered into force for a Party, that Party may withdraw from the Convention by giving written notification to the Depositary.
2. Any such withdrawal shall take effect upon expiry of one year from the date of receipt by the Depositary of the notification of withdrawal, or on such later date as may be specified in the notification of withdrawal.

Article 39. Depositary

The Secretary General of the United Nations shall be the Depositary of the Convention.

Article 40. Authentic Texts

The original of the present Convention, of which the Arabic, Chinese, English, French, Russian and Spanish texts are equally authentic, shall be deposited with the Secretary General of the United Nations.

In witness whereof the undersigned, being duly authorized to that effect, have signed the present Convention.

Done at Paris, this 17th day of June one thousand nine hundred and ninety-four.

ANNEX 1

REGIONAL IMPLEMENTATION ANNEX FOR AFRICA

Article 1. Scope

This Annex applies to Africa, in relation to each Party and in conformity with the Convention, in particular its article 7, for the purpose of combating desertification and/or mitigating the effects of drought in its arid, semi arid and dry sub-humid areas.

Article 2. Purpose

The purpose of this Annex, at the national, subregional and regional levels in Africa and in the light of its particular conditions, is to:

(a) identify measures and arrangements, including the nature and processes of assistance provided by developed country Parties, in accordance with the relevant provisions of the Conventions;

(b) provide for the efficient and practical implementation of the Convention to address conditions specific to Africa; and

(c) promote processes and activities relating to combating desertification and/or mitigating the effects of drought within the arid, semi-arid and dry sub-humid areas of Africa.

Article 3. Particular Conditions of the African Region

In carrying out their obligations under the Convention, the Parties shall, in the implementation of this Annex, adopt a basic approach that takes into consideration the following particular conditions of Africa:

(a) the high proportion of arid, semi-arid and dry sub-humid areas;

(b) the substantial number of countries and populations adversely affected by desertification and by the frequent recurrence of severe drought;

(c) the large number of affected countries that are land-locked;

(d) the widespread poverty prevalent in most affected countries, the large number of least developed countries among them, and their need for significant amounts of external assistance, in the form of grants and loans on concessional terms, to pursue their developed objectives;

(e) the difficult socio-economic conditions, exacerbated by deteriorating and fluctuating terms of trade, external indebtedness and political instability, which induce internal, regional and international migrations;

(f) the heavy reliance of populations on natural resources for subsistence which, compounded by the effects of demographic trends and factors, a weak technological base and unsustainable production practices, contributes to serious resource degradation;

(g) the insufficient institutional and legal frameworks, the weak infrastructural base and the insufficient scientific, technical and educational capacity, leading to substantial capacity building requirements; and

(h) the central role of actions to combat desertification and/or mitigate the effects of drought in the national development priorities of affected African countries.

Article 4. Commitments and Obligations of African Country Parties

1. In accordance with their respective capabilities, African country Parties undertake to:

(a) adopt the combating of desertification and/or the mitigation of the effects of drought as a central strategy in their efforts to eradicate poverty;

(b) promote regional cooperation and integration, in a spirit of solidarity and partnership based on mutual interest, in programmes and activities to combat desertification and/or mitigate the effects of drought;

(c) rationalize and strengthen existing institutions concerned with desertification and drought and involve other existing institutions, as appropriate, in order to make them more effective and to ensure more efficient use of resources;

(d) promote the exchange of information on appropriate technology, knowledge, know-how and practice between and among them; and

(e) develop contingency plans for mitigating the effects of drought in areas degraded by desertification and/or drought.

2. Pursuant to the general and specific obligations set out in articles 4 and 5 of the Convention, affected African country Parties shall aim to:

(a) make appropriate financial allocations from their national budgets consistent with national conditions and capabilities and reflecting the new priority Africa has accorded to the phenomenon of desertification and/or drought;

(b) sustain and strengthen reforms currently in progress towards greater decentralization and resource tenure as well as reinforce participation of local populations and communities.

Article 5. Strategic Planning Framework for Sustainable Development

1. National action programmes shall be a central and integral part of a broader process of formulating national policies for the sustainable development of affected African country Parties.
2. A consultative and participatory process involving appropriate levels of government, local populations, communities and non-governmental organizations shall be undertaken to provide guidance on a strategy with flexible planning to allow maximum participation from local populations and communities. As appropriate, bilateral and multilateral assistance agencies may be involved in this process at the request of an affected African country Party.

Article 6. Timetable for Preparation of Action Programmes

Pending entry into force of this Convention, the African country Parties, in cooperation with other members of the international community, as appropriate, shall, to the extent possible, provisionally apply those provisions of the Convention relating to the preparation of national, subregional and regional action programmes.

Article 7. Content of National Action Programmes

1. Consistent with Article 10 of the Convention, the overall strategy of national action programmes shall emphasize integrated local development programmes for affected areas, based on participatory mechanisms and on integration of strategies for poverty eradication into efforts to combat desertification and mitigate the effects of drought. The programmes shall aim at strengthening the capacity of local authorities and ensuring the active involvement of local populations, communities and groups, with emphasis on education and training, mobilization of non governmental organizations with proven expertise and strengthening of decentralized governmental structures.
2. National action programmes shall, as appropriate, include the following general features:
   (a) the use, in developing and implementing national action programmes, of past experiences in combating desertification and/or mitigating the effects of drought, taking into account social, economic and ecological conditions;
   (b) the identification of factors contributing to desertification and/or drought and the resources and capacities available and required, and the setting up of appropriate policies and institutional and other responses and measures necessary to combat those phenomena and/or mitigate their effects; and

(c) the increase in participation of local populations and communities, including women, farmers and pastoralists, and delegation to them of more responsibility for management.

3. National action programmes shall also, as appropriate, include the following:

(a) measures to improve the economic environment with a view to eradicating poverty:

(i) increasing incomes and employment opportunities, especially for the poorest members of the community, by developing markets for farm and livestock products; creating financial instruments suited to local needs; encouraging diversification in agriculture and the setting up of agricultural enterprises; and developing economic activities of a para-agricultural or non-agricultural type;

(ii) improving the long-term prospects of rural economics by the creation of incentives for productive investment and access to the means of production; and price and tax policies and commercial practices that promote growth;

(iii) defining and applying population and migration policies to reduce population pressure on land; and

(iv) promoting the use of drought resistant crops and the application of integrated dry land farming systems for food security purposes.

(b) measures to conserve natural resources:

(i) ensuring integrated and sustainable management of natural resources, including agricultural, land and pastoral land, vegetation cover and wildlife forests, water resources, and biological diversity;

(ii) training with regard to, and strengthening, public awareness and environmental education campaigns and disseminating knowledge of techniques relating to the sustainable management of natural resources; and

(iii) ensuring the development and efficient use of diverse energy sources, the promotion of alternative sources of energy, particularly solar energy, wind energy and bio-gas, and specific arrangements for the transfer, acquisition and adaptation of relevant technology to alleviate the pressure on fragile natural resources;

(c) measures to improve institutional organization:

(i) defining the roles and responsibilities of central governmental and local authorities within the framework of a land use planning policy;

(ii) encouraging a policy of active decentralization, devolving responsibility for management and decision making to local authorities, and encouraging initiatives and the assumption of responsibility by local communities and the establishment of local structures; and

(iii) adjusting, as appropriate, the institutional and regulatory framework of natural resource management to provide security of land tenure for local populations;

(d) measures to improve knowledge of desertification:

(i) promoting research and the collection, processing and exchange of information on the scientific, technical and socio-economic aspects of desertification;

(ii) improving national capabilities in research and in the collection, processing, exchange and analysis of information so as to increase understanding and to translate the results of the analysis into operational terms; and

(iii) encouraging the medium and long term study of:

socio-economic and cultural trends in affected areas; qualitative and quantitative trends in natural resources; and the interaction between climate and desertification; and

(e) measures to monitor and assess the effects of drought:

(i) developing strategies to evaluate the impacts of natural climate variability on regional drought and desertification and/or to utilize predictions of climate variability on seasonal to interannual time scales in efforts to mitigate the effects of drought;

(ii) improving early warning and response capacity, efficiently managing emergency relief and food aid, and improving food stocking and distribution systems, cattle protection schemes and public works and alternative livelihoods for drought prone areas; and

(iii) monitoring and assessing ecological degradation to provide reliable and timely information on the process and dynamics of resource degradation in order to facilitate better policy formulations and responses.

Article 8. Preparation of National Action Programmes and Implementation and Evaluation Indicators

Each affected African country Party shall designate an appropriate national coordinate body to function as a catalyst in the preparation, implementation and evaluation of its national action programme. This coordinating body shall, in the light of Article 3, as appropriate:

(a) undertake an identification and review of actions, beginning with locally driven consultation process, involving local populations and communities and with the cooperation of local administrative authorities, developed country Parties and intergovernmental and non-governmental organizations, on the basis of initial consultations of those concerned at the national level;

(b) identify and analyze the constraints, needs and gaps

affecting development and sustainable land use and recommend practical measures to avoid duplication by making full use of relevant ongoing efforts and promote implementation of results;

(c) facilitate, design and formulate project activities based on interactive, flexible approaches in order to ensure active participation of the population in affected areas, to minimize the negative impact of such activities, and to identify and prioritize requirements for financial assistance and technical cooperation.

(d) establish pertinent, quantifiable and readily verifiable indicators to ensure the assessment and evaluation of national action programmes, which encompass actions in the short, medium and long terms, and of the implementation of such programmes; and

(e) prepare progress reports on the implementation of the national action programmes.

Article 9. Organizational Framework of Subregional Action Programmes

1. Pursuant to Article 4 of the Convention, African country Parties shall cooperate in the preparation and implementation of subregional action programmes for central, eastern, northern, southern and western Africa and, in that regard, may delegate the following responsibilities to relevant subregional intergovernmental organizations:

(a) acting as focal points for preparatory activities and coordinating the implementation of the subregional action programmes;

(b) assisting in the preparation and implementation of national action programmes;

(c) facilitating the exchange of information, experience and know-how as well as providing advice on the review of national legislation; and

(d) any other responsibilities relating to the implementation of subregional action programmes.

2. Specialized subregional institutions may provide support, upon request, and/or be entrusted with the responsibility to coordinate activities in their respective fields of competence.

Article 10. Content and Preparation of Subregional Action Programmes

Subregional action programmes shall focus on issues that are better addressed at the subregional level. They shall establish, where necessary, mechanisms for the management of shares natural resources. Such mechanisms shall effectively handle transboundary problems associated with desertification and/or drought and shall provide support for the harmonious implementation of national action programmes. Priority areas for subregional action programmes shall, as appropriate, focus on:

(a) joint programmes for the sustainable management of transboundary natural resources through bilateral and multilateral mechanisms, as appropriate;

(b) coordination of programmes to develop alternative energy sources;

(c) cooperation in the management and control of pests as well as of plant and animal diseases;

(d) capacity building, education and public awareness activities that are better carried out or supported at the subregional level;

(e) scientific and technical cooperation, particularly in the climatological, meteorological and hydrological fields, including networking for data collection and assessment, information sharing and project monitoring, and coordination and prioritization of research and development activities;

(f) early warning systems and joint planning for mitigating the effects of drought, including measures to address the problems resulting from environmentally induced migrations;

(g) exploration of ways of sharing experiences, particularly regarding participation of local populations and communities, and creation of an enabling environment for improved land use management and for use of appropriate technologies;

(h) strengthening of the capacity of subregional organizations to coordinate and provide technical services, as well as establishment, reorientation and strengthening of subregional centres and institutions; and

(i) development of policies in fields, such as trade, which have impact upon affected areas and populations, including policies for the coordination of regional marketing regimes and for common infrastructure.

Article 11. Organizational Framework of the Regional Action Programmes

1. Pursuant to Article 11 of the Convention, African country Parties shall jointly determine the procedures for preparing and implementing the regional action programme.
2. The Parties may provide appropriate support to relevant African regional institutions and organizations to enable them to assist African country Parties to fulfil their responsibilities under the Convention.

Article 12. Content of the Regional Action Programme

The regional action programme includes measures relating to combating desertification and/or mitigating the effects of drought in the following priority areas, as appropriate:

(a) development of regional cooperation and coordination of sub-regional action programmes for building regional consensus on key policy areas, including through regular consultations of sub-regional organizations;

(b) promotion of capacity building in activities which are better implemented at the regional level;

(c) the seeking of solutions with the international community to global economic and social issues that have an impact on affected areas taking into account Article 4, paragraph 2(b) of the Convention;

(d) promotion among the affected country Parties of Africa and its subregions, as well as with other affected regions, of exchange of information and appropriate techniques, technical know-how and relevant experience; promotion of scientific and technological cooperation particularly in the fields of climatology, meteorology, hydrology, water resource development and alternative energy sources; coordination of sub-regional land regional research activities; and identification of regional priorities for research and development;

(e) coordination of networks for systematic observation and assessment and information exchange, as well as their integration into world wide networks; and

(f) coordination of and reinforcement of sub-regional and regional early warning systems and drought contingency plans.

Article 13. Financial Resources

1. Pursuant to Article 20 of the Convention and Article 4, paragraph 2, affected African country Parties shall endeavour to provide a macroeconomic framework conducive to channel resources more effectively to local development programmes, including through non-governmental organizations, as appropriate.
2. Pursuant to Article 21, paragraphs 4 and 5 of the Convention, the Parties agree to establish an inventory of sources of funding at the national, subregional and international levels to ensure the rational use of existing resources and to identify gaps in resource allocation, to facilitate implementation of the action programmes. The inventory shall be regularly reviewed and updated.

3. Consistent with Article 7 of the Convention, the developed country Parties shall continue to allocate significant resources and/or increased resources as well as other forms of assistance to affected African country Parties on the basis of partnership agreements and arrangements referred to in Article 18, giving, *inter alia,* due attention to matters related to debt, international trade and marketing arrangements in accordance with Article 4, paragraph 2(b) of the Convention.

Article 14. Financial Mechanisms

1. Consistent with Article 7 of the Convention underscoring the priority to affected African country Parties and considering the particular situation prevailing in this region, the Parties shall pay special attention to the implementation in Africa of the provisions of Article 21, paragraph 1 (d) and (e) of the Convention, notably by :
   (a) facilitating the establishment of mechanisms, such as national desertification funds, to channel financial resources to the local level; and
   (b) strengthening existing funds and financial mechanisms at the subregional and regional levels.
2. Consistent with Articles 20 and 21 of the Convention, the Parties which are also members of the governing bodies of relevant regional and subregional financial institutions, including the African Development Bank and the African Development Fund, shall promote efforts to give due priority and attention to the activities of those institutions that advance the implementation of this Annex.
3. The Parties shall streamline, to the extent possible, procedures for channelling funds to affected African country Parties.

Article 15. Technical Assistance and Cooperation

The Parties undertake, in accordance with their respective

capabilities, to rationalize technical assistance to, and cooperation with, African country Parties with a view to increasing project and programme effectiveness by, *inter alia:*

(a) limiting the costs of support measures and backstopping, especially overhead costs; in any case, such costs shall only represent an appropriately low percentage of the total cost of the project so as to maximize project efficiency;

(b) giving preference to the utilization of competent national experts or, where necessary, competent experts from within the subregion and/or region, in project design, preparation and implementation, and to the building of local expertise where it does not exist; and

(c) effectively managing and coordinating, as well as efficiently utilizing, technical assistance to be provided.

Article 16. Transfer, Acquisition, Adaptation and Access to Environmentally Sound Technology

In implementing Article 18 of the Convention relating to transfer, adaptation and development of technology, the Parties undertake to give priority to African country Parties and, as necessary to develop with them new models of partnership and cooperation with a view to strengthening capacity building in the fields of scientific research and development and information collection and dissemination to enable them to implement their strategies to combat desertification and mitigate the effects of drought.

Article 17. Coordination and Partnership Agreements

1. African country Parties shall coordinate the preparation, negotiation and implementation of national, subregional and regional action programmes. They may involve, as appropriate, other Parties and relevant intergovernmental and non-governmental organizations in this process.
2. The objectives of such coordination shall be to ensure that financial and technical cooperation is consistent with the

Convention and to provide the necessary continuity in the use and administration of resources.

3. African country Parties shall organize consultative processes at the national, subregional and regional levels. These consultative processes may:
   (a) serve as a forum to negotiate and conclude partnership agreements based on national, subregional and regional action programmes; and
   (b) specify the contribution of African country Parties and other members of the consultative groups to the programmes and identify priorities and agreements on implementation and evaluation indicators, as well as funding arrangements for implementation.
4. The Permanent Secretariat may, at the request of African country Parties, pursuant to Article 23 of the Convention, facilitate the convocation of such consultative processes by:
   (a) providing advice on the organization of effective consultative arrangements, drawing on experiences from other such arrangements;
   (b) providing information to relevant bilateral and multilateral agencies concerning consultative meetings or processes, and encouraging their active involvement; and
   (c) providing other information that may be relevant in establishing or improving consultative arrangements.
5. The subregional and regional coordinating bodies shall, *inter alia*:
   (a) recommend appropriate adjustments to partnership agreements;
   (b) monitor, assess and report on the implementation of the agreed subregional and regional programmes; and
   (c) aim to ensure efficient communication and cooperation among African country Parties.
6. Participation in the consultative groups shall, as

appropriate, be open to Governments, interested groups and donors, relevant organs, funds and programmes of the United Nations system, relevant subregional and regional organizations, and representatives of relevant non-governmental organizations. Participants of each consultative group shall determine the modalities of its management and operation.

7. Pursuant to Article 14 of the Convention, developed country Parties are encouraged to develop, on their own initiative, an informal process of consultation and coordination among themselves, at the national, subregional and regional levels, and at the request of an affected African country Party or of an appropriate subregional or regional organization, to participate in a national, subregional or regional consultative process that would evaluate and respond to assistance needs in order to facilitate implementation.

Article 18. Follow-up Arrangements

Follow-up of this Annex shall be carried out by African country Parties in accordance with the Convention as follows:

(a) at the national level, by a mechanism the composition of which should be determined by each affected African country Party and which shall include representatives of local communities and shall function under the supervision of the national coordinating body referred to in Article 9.

(b) at the subregional level, by a multidisciplinary scientific and technical consultative committee, the composition and modalities of operation of which shall be determined by the African country Parties of the subregion concerned; and

(c) at the regional level, by mechanisms defined in accordance with the relevant provisions of the Treaty establishing the African Economic

Community, and by an African Scientific and Technical Advisory Committee.

ANNEX II

REGIONAL IMPLEMENTATION ANNEX FOR ASIA

Article 1. Purpose

The purpose of this Annex is to provide guidelines and arrangements for the effective implementation of the Convention in the affected country Parties of the Asian region in the light of its particular conditions.

Article 2. Particular Conditions of the Asian Region

In carrying out their obligations under the Convention, the Parties shall, as appropriate, take into consideration the following particular conditions which apply in varying degrees to the affected country Parties of the region:

(a) the high proportion of areas in their territories affected by, or vulnerable to, desertification and drought and the broad diversity of these areas with regard to climate, topography land use and socio-economic systems;

(b) the heavy pressure on natural resources for livelihoods;

(c) the existence of production systems, directly related to widespread poverty, leading to land degradation and to pressure on scarce water resources;

(d) the significant impact of conditions in the world economy and social problems such as poverty, poor health and nutrition, lack of food security, migration, displaced persons and demographic dynamics;

(e) their expanding, but still insufficient, capacity and institutional frameworks to deal with national desertification and drought problems; and

(f) their need for international cooperation to pursue sustainable development objectives relating to combating desertification and mitigating the effects of drought.

Article 3. Framework for National Action Programmes

1. National action programmes shall be an integral part of broader national policies for sustainable development of the affected country Parties of the region.
2. The affected country Parties shall, as appropriate, develop national action programmes pursuant to Articles 9 to 11 of the Convention, paying special attention to Article 10, paragraph 2(f). As appropriate, bilateral and multilateral cooperation agencies may be involved in this process at the request of the affected country Party concerned.

Article 4. National Action Programmes

1. In preparing and implementing national action programmes, the affected country Parties of the region, consistent with their respective circumstances and policies, may, *inter alia,* as appropriate:
   (a) designate appropriate bodies responsible for the preparation, coordination and implementation of their action programmes;
   (b) involve affected populations, including local communities, in the elaboration, coordination and implementation of their action programmes through a locally driven consultative process, with the cooperation of local authorities and relevant national and non-governmental organizations;
   (c) survey the state of the environment in affected areas to assess the causes and consequences of desertification and to determine priority areas for action;
   (d) evaluate, with the participation of affected populations, past and current programmes for combating desertification and mitigating the effects of drought, in order to design a strategy and elaborate activities in their action programmes;

(e) prepare technical and financial programmes based on the information derived from the activities in subparagraphs (a) to (d);
(f) develop and utilize procedures and benchmarks for evaluating implementation of their action programmes;
(g) promote the integrated management of drainage basins, the conservation of soil resources, and the enhancement and efficient use of water resources;
(h) strengthen and/or establish information, evaluation and follow up and early warning systems in regions prone to desertification and drought, taking account of climatological, meteorological, hydrological, biological and other relevant factors; and
(i) formulate in a spirit of partnership where international cooperation, including financial and technical resources, is involved, appropriate arrangements supporting their action programmes.

2. Consistent with Article 10 of the Convention, the overall strategy of national action programmes shall emphasize integrated local development programmes for affected areas, based on participatory mechanisms and on the integration of strategies for poverty eradication into efforts to combat desertification and mitigate the effects of drought. Sectoral measures in the action programmes shall be grouped in priority fields which take account of the broad diversity of affected areas in the region referred to in Article 2(a).

Article 5. Subregional and Joint Action Programmes

1. Pursuant to Article 11 of the Convention, affected country Parties in Asia may mutually agree to consult and cooperate with other Parties, as appropriate, to prepare and implement subregional or joint action programmes, as appropriate, in order to complement, and increase effectiveness in the implementation of, national action

programmes. In either case, the relevant Parties may jointly agree to entrust subregional, including bilateral or national organizations, or specialized institutions, with responsibilities relating to the preparation, coordination and implementation of programmes. Such organizations or institutions may also act as focal points for the promotion and coordination of actions pursuant to Articles 16 to 18 of the Convention.

2. In preparing and implementing subregional or joint action programmes, the affected country Parties of the region shall, *inter alia,* as appropriate:
   (a) identify, in cooperation with national institutions, priorities relating to combating desertification and mitigating the effects of drought which can better be met by such programmes, as well as relevant activities which could be effectively carried out through them;
   (b) evaluate the operational capacities and activities of relevant regional, subregional and national institutions;
   (c) assess existing programmes relating to desertification and drought among all or some parties of the region or subregion and their relationship with national action programmes; and
   (d) formulate in a spirit of partnership, where international cooperation, including financial and technical resources, is involved, appropriate bilateral and/or multilateral arrangements supporting the programmes.
3. Subregional or joint action programmes may include agreed joint programmes for the sustainable management of transboundary natural resources relating to desertification, priorities for coordination and other activities in the fields of capacity building, scientific and technical cooperation, particularly drought early warning systems and information sharing, and means of strengthening the relevant subregional and other organizations or institutions:

Article 6. Regional Activities

Regional activities for the enhancement of subregional or joint action programmes may include, *inter alia*, measures to strengthen institutions and mechanisms for coordination and cooperation at the national, subregional and regional levels, and to promote the implementation of Articles 16 to 19 of the Convention. These activities may also include:

(a) promoting and strengthening technical cooperation networks;

(b) preparing inventories of technologies, knowledge, know-how and practices, as well as

(c) evaluating the requirements for technology transfer and promoting the adaptation and use of such technologies; and

(d) encouraging public awareness programmes and promoting capacity building at all levels, strengthening training, research and development and building systems for human resource development.

Article 7. Financial Resources and Mechanisms

1. The Parties shall, in view of the importance of combating desertification and mitigating the effects of drought in the Asian region, promote the mobilization of substantial financial resources and the availability of financial mechanisms, pursuant to Articles 20 and 21 of the Convention.
2. In conformity with the Convention and on the basis of the coordinating mechanism provided for in Article 8 and in accordance with their national development policies, affected country Parties of the region shall, individually or jointly:

   (a) adopt measures to rationalize and strengthen mechanisms to supply funds through public and private investment with a view to achieving specific results in action to combat desertification and mitigate the effects of drought;

(b) identify international cooperation requirements in support of national efforts, particularly financial, technical and technological; and

(c) promote the participation of bilateral and/or multilateral financial cooperation institutions with a view to ensuring implementation of the Convention.

3. The Parties shall streamline, to the extent possible, procedures for channelling funds to affected country Parties in the region.

Article 8. Cooperation and Coordination Mechanisms

1. Affected country Parties, through the appropriate bodies designated pursuant to Article 4, paragraph 1 (a), and other Parties in the region, may, as appropriate, set up a mechanism for, *inter alia,* the following purposes:

(a) exchange of information, experience, knowledge and know-how;

(b) cooperation and coordination of actions, including bilateral and multilateral arrangements at the subregional and regional levels;

(c) promotion of scientific, technical, technological and financial cooperation pursuant to Articles 5 to 7;

(d) identification of external cooperation requirements; and

(e) follow-up and evaluation of the implementation of action programmes.

2. Affected country Parties, through the appropriate bodies designated pursuant to Article 4, paragraph 1 (a), and other Parties in the region, may also, as appropriate, consult and coordinate as regards the national, subregional and joint action programmes. They may involve, as appropriate, other Parties and relevant intergovernmental and non governmental organizations in this process. Such coordination shall, *inter alia,* seek to secure agreement on

opportunities for international cooperation in accordance with Articles 20 and 21 of the Convention, enhance technical cooperation and channel resources so that they are used effectively.

3. Affected country Parties of the region shall hold periodic coordination meetings, and the Permanent Secretariat may, at their request, pursuant to Article 23 of the Convention, facilitate the convocation of such coordination meetings by:
   (a) providing advice on the organization of effective coordination arrangements, drawing on experience from other such arrangements;
   (b) providing information to relevant bilateral and multilateral agencies concerning coordination meetings, and encouraging their active involvement; and
   (c) providing other information that may be relevant in establishing or improving coordination processes.

ANNEX III

REGIONAL IMPLEMENTATION ANNEX FOR LATIN AMERICA AND THE CARIBBEAN

Article 1. Purpose

The purpose of this Annex is to provide general guidelines for the implementation of the Convention in the Latin American and Caribbean region, in light of its particular conditions.

Article 2. Particular Conditions of the Latin America

The Parties shall, in accordance with the provisions of the Convention, take into consideration the following particular conditions of the region:

(a) the existence of broad expanses which are vulnerable and have been severely affected by desertification and/or drought and in which diverse characteristics may be observed, depending on the area in which they occur;

this cumulative and intensifying process has negative social, cultural, economic and environmental effects which are all the more serious in that the region contains one of the largest resources of biological diversity in the world;

(b) the frequent use of unsustainable development practices in affected areas as a result of complex interactions among physical, biological, political, social, cultural and economic factors, including international economic factors such as external indebtedness, deteriorating terms of trade and trade practices which affect markets for agricultural, fishery and forestry products; and

(c) a sharp drop in the productivity of ecosystems being the main consequence of desertification and drought, taking the form of a decline in agricultural, livestock and forestry yields and a loss of biological diversity; from the social point of view, the results are impoverishment, migration, internal population movements, and the deterioration of the quality of life; the region will therefore have to adopt an integrated approach to problems of desertification and drought by promoting sustainable development models that are in keeping with the environmental, economic and social situation in each country.

Article 3. Action Programmes

1. In conformity with the Convention, in particular its Articles 9 to 11, and in accordance with their national development policies, affected country Parties of the region shall, as appropriate, prepare and implement national action programmes to combat desertification and mitigate the effects of drought as an integral part of their national policies for sustainable development. Subregional and regional programmes may be prepared and implemented in accordance with the requirements of the region.

2. In the preparation of their national action programmes, affected country Parties of the region shall pay particular attention to Article 10, paragraph 2 (f) of the Convention.

Article 4. Content of National Action Programmes

In the light of their respective situations, the affected country Parties of the region may take account, *inter alia*, of the following thematic issues in developing their national strategies for action to combat desertification and/or mitigate the effects of drought, pursuant to Article 5 of the Convention:

(a) increasing capacities, education and public awareness, technical, scientific and technological cooperation and financial resources and mechanisms;
(b) eradicating poverty and improving the quality of human life;
(c) achieving food security and sustainable development and management of agricultural, livestock-rearing, forestry and multipurpose activities;
(d) sustainable management of natural resources, especially the rational management of drainage basins;
(e) sustainable management of natural resources in high altitude areas;
(f) rational management and conservation of soil resources and exploitation and efficient use of water resources;
(g) formulation and application of emergency plans to mitigate the effects of drought;
(h) strengthening and/or establishing information, evaluation and follow-up and early warning systems in areas prone to desertification and drought, taking account of climatological, meteorological, hydrological, biological, soil, economic and social factors;
(i) developing, managing and efficiently using diverse sources of energy, including promotion of alternative sources;

(j) conservation and sustainable use of biodiversity in accordance with the provisions of the Convention on Biological Diversity;

(k) consideration of demographic aspects related to desertification and drought; and

(l) establishing or strengthening institutional and legal frameworks permitting application of the Convention and aimed, *inter alia,* at decentralizing administrative structures and functions relating to desertification and drought, with the participation of affected communities and society in general.

Article 5. Technical, Scientific and Technological Cooperation

In conformity with the Convention, in particular its Articles 16 to 18, and on the basis of the coordinating mechanisms provided for in Article 7, affected country Parties of the region shall, individually or jointly:

(a) promote the strengthening of technical cooperation networks and national, subregional and regional information systems, as well as their integration, as appropriate, in worldwide sources of information:

(b) prepare an inventory of available technologies and know-how and promote their dissemination and use;

(c) promote the use of traditional technology, knowledge, know-how and practices pursuant to Article 18, paragraph 2 (b), of the Convention;

(d) identify transfer of technology requirements; and

(e) promote the development, adaptation, adoption and transfer of relevant existing and new environmentally sound technologies.

Article 6. Financial Resources and Mechanisms

In conformity with the Convention, in particular its Articles 20 and 21, on the basis of the coordinating mechanism provided for in Article 7 and in accordance with their national development policies, affected country Parties of the region shall, individually or jointly:

(a) adopt measures to rationalize and strengthen mechanisms to supply funds through public and private investments with a view to achieving specific results in action to combat desertification and mitigate the effects of drought;

(b) identify international cooperation requirements in support of national efforts; and

(c) promote the participation of bilateral and/or multilateral financial cooperation institutions with a view to ensuring implementation of the Convention.

Article 7. Institutional Framework

1. In order to give effect to this Annex, affected country Parties of the region shall:

   (a) establish and/or strengthen national focal points to coordinate action to combat desertification and/or mitigate the effects of drought; and

   (b) set up a mechanism to coordinate the national focal points for the following purposes:

      (i) exchanges of information and experience;

      (ii) coordination of activities at the subregional and regional levels;

      (iii) promotion of technical, scientific, technological and financial cooperation.

      (iv) identification of external cooperation requirements; and

      (v) follow-up and evaluation of the implementation of action programmes.

2. Affected country Parties of the region shall hold periodic coordination meetings and the Permanent Secretariat may, at their request, pursuant to Article 23 of the Convention, facilitate the convention of such coordination meetings, by:

(a) providing advice on the organization of effective coordination arrangements, drawing on experience from other such arrangements;

(b) providing information to relevant bilateral and multilateral agencies coordination meetings, and encouraging their active involvement; and

(c) providing other information that may be relevant in establishing or improving coordination processes.

ANNEX IV

REGIONAL IMPLEMENTATION ANNEX FOR THE NORTHERN MEDITERRANEAN

Article 1. Purpose

The purpose of this Annex is to provide guidelines and arrangements necessary for the effective implementation of the Conventions in affected country Parties of the northern Mediterranean region in the light of its particular conditions.

Article 2. Particular Conditions of the Northern Mediterranean Region

The particular conditions of the northern Mediterranean region referred to in Article 1 include:

(a) semi arid climatic conditions affecting large areas, seasonal droughts, very high rainfall variability and sudden and high intensity rainfall;

(b) poor and highly erodible soils, prone to develop surface crusts;

(c) uneven relief with steep slopes and very diversified landscapes;

(d) extensive forest coverage losses due to frequent wildfires;

(e) crisis conditions in traditional agriculture with associated land abandonment and deterioration of soil and water conservation structures;

(f) unsustainable exploitation of water resources leading to serious environmental damage, including chemical pollution, salinization and exhaustion of aquifers; and
(g) concentration of economic activity in coastal areas as a result of urban growth, industrial activities, tourism and irrigated agriculture.

Article 3. Strategic Planning Framework for Sustainable Development

1. National action programmes shall be a central and integral part of the strategic planning framework for sustainable development of the affected country Parties of the northern Mediterranean.
2. A consultative and participatory process, involving appropriate levels of government, local communities and nongovernmental organizations, shall be undertaken to provide guidance on a strategy with flexible planning to allow maximum local participation, pursuant to article 10, paragraph 2 (f) of the Convention.

Article 4. Obligation to Prepare National Action Programmes and Timetable

Affected country Parties of the northern Mediterranean region shall prepare national action programmes and, as appropriate, subregional, regional or joint actions programmes. The preparation of such programmes shall be finalized as soon as practicable.

Article 5. Preparation and Implementation of National Action Programmes

In preparing and implementing national action programmes pursuant to Articles 9 and 10 of the Convention, each affected country Party of the region shall, as appropriate:

(a) designate appropriate bodies responsible for the

preparation, coordination and implementation of its programmes;

(b) involve affected populations, including local communities, in the elaboration, coordination and implementation of the programme through a locally driven consultative process, with the cooperation of local authorities and relevant non-governmental organizations;

(c) survey the state of the environment in affected areas to assess the causes and consequences of desertification and to determine priority areas for action;

(d) evaluate, with the participation of affected populations, past and current programmes in order to design a strategy and elaborate activities in the action programme;

(e) prepare technical land financial programmes based on the information gained through the activities in subparagraphs (a) to (d); and

(f) develop and utilize procedures and benchmarks for monitoring and evaluating the implementation of the programme.

Article 6. Content of National Action Programmes

Affected country Parties of the region may include, in their national action programmes, measures relating to:

(a) legislative, institutional and administrative areas;

(b) land use patterns, management of water resources, soil conservation, forestry, agricultural activities and pasture and range management;

(c) management and conservation of wildlife and other forms of biological diversity;

(d) protection against forest fires;

(e) promotion of alternative livelihoods; and

(f) research, training and public awareness.

Article 7. Subregional, Regional and Joint Action Programmes

1. Affected country Parties of the region may, in accordance with Article 11 of the Convention, prepare and implement subregional and/or regional action programmes in order to complement and increase the efficiency of national action programmes. Two or more affected country Parties of the region, may similarly agree to prepare a joint action programme between or among them.
2. The provisions of Articles 5 and 6 shall apply *mutatis mutandis* to the preparation and implementation of sub-regional, regional and joint action programmes. In addition, such programmes may include the conduct of research and development activities concerning selected ecosystems in affected areas.
3. In preparing and implementing subregional, regional or joint action programmes, affected country Parties of the region shall, as appropriate:
   (a) identify, in cooperation with national institutions, national objectives relating to desertification which can better be met by such programmes and relevant activities which could be effectively carried out through them;
   (b) evaluate the operational capacities and activities of relevant regional, subregional and national institutions; and
   (c) assess existing programmes relating to desertification among Parties of the region and their relationship with national action programmes.

Article 8. Coordination of Subregional, Regional and Joint Action Programmes

Affected country Parties preparing a subregional, regional or joint action programme may establish a coordination committee composed of representatives of each affected country Party concerned to review progress in combating desertification, harmonize national action programmes, make recommendations at the various stages of preparation and implementation of the subregional, regional or joint action programme, and act as a focal point for the promotion and coordination of technical cooperation pursuant to Articles 16 to 19 of the Convention.

Article 9. Non-eligibility for Financial Assistance

In implementing national, subregional, regional and joint action programmes, affected developed country Parties of the region are not eligible to receive financial assistance under this Convention.

Article 10. Coordination with Other Subregions and Regions

Subregional, regional and joint action programmes in the northern Mediterranean region may be prepared and implemented in collaboration with those of other subregions or regions, particularly with those of the subregion of northern Africa.

APPENDIX II

Convention on Biological Diversity

UNITED NATIONS CONVENTION ON BIOLOGICAL DIVERSITY

PREAMBLE

The Contracting Parties,

Conscious of the intrinsic value of biological diversity and of the ecological, genetic, social, economic, scientific, educational, cultural, recreational and aesthetic values of biological diversity and its components,

Conscious also of the importance of biological diversity for evolution and for maintaining life sustaining systems of the biosphere,

Affirming that the conservation biological diversity is a common concern of humankind,

Reaffirming that States have sovereign rights over their own biological resources,

Reaffirming also that states are responsible for conserving their biological diversity and for using their biological resources in a sustainable manner,

Concerned that biological diversity is being significantly reduced by certain human activities,

Aware of the general lack of information and knowledge regarding biological diversity and for the urgent need to develop scientific, technical and institutional capacities to provide the basic understanding upon which to plan and implement appropriate measures,

Noting that it is vital to anticipate, prevent and attack the causes of significant reduction or loss of biological diversity at source,

Noting also that where there is a threat of significant reduction or loss of biological diversity, lack of full scientific cetainty should not be used as a reason for postponing measures to avoid or minimize such a threat,

Noting further that the fundamental requirement for the conservation of biological diversity is the in-situ conservation of ecosystems and natural habitats and the maintenance and recovery of viable populations of species in their natural surroundings,

Noting further that ex-situ measures, preferably in the country of origin, also have an important role to play,

Recognizing the close and traditional dependence of many indigenous and local communities embodying traditional lifestyles on biological resources, and the desirability or sharing equitably benefits arising from the use of traditional knowledge, innovations and practices relevant to the conservation of biological diversity and the sustainable use of its components,

Recognizing also the vital role that women play in the conservation and sustainable use of biological diversity and affirming the need for the full participation of women at all levels of policy-making and implementation for biological diversity conservation,

Stressing the importance of and the need to promote, international, regional and global cooperation among States and intergovernmental organizations and the non-governmental sector for the conservation of biological diversity and the sustainable use of its components,

Acknowledging that the provision of new and additional financial resources and appropriate access to relevant technologies can be expected to make a substantial difference in the world's ability to address the loss of biological diversity,

Acknowledging further that special provision is required to meet the needs of developing countries, including the provision of new and additional financial resources and appropriate access to relevant technologies,

Noting in this regard the special condition of the least developed countries and small island States,

Acknowledging that substantial investments are required to conserve biologically diversity and that there is the expectation of a broad range of environmental, economic and social benefits from those investments,

Recognizing that economic and social development and poverty eradication are the first and overriding priorities of developing countries,

Aware that conservation and sustainable use of biological diversity is of critical importance for meeting the food, health and other needs of the growing world population, for which purpose access to and sharing of both genetic resources and technologies are essential,

Noting that, ultimately, the conservation and sustainable use of biological diversity will strength friendly relations among States and contribute to peace for humankind,

Desiring to enhance and complement existing international arrangements for the conservation of biological diversity and sustainable use of its components, and

Determined to conserve and sustainable use of biological diversity for the benefit of present and future generations,

Have agreed as follows:

Article 1. Objectives

The objectives of this Convention, to be pursued in accordance with its relevant provision, are the conservation of biological diversity, the sustainable use of its components and the fair and equitable sharing of the benefits arising out of the utilization of genetic resources, including by appropriate access to genetic resources and by appropriate transfer of relevant technologies, taking into account all rights over those resources and to technologies, and by appropriate funding.

Article 2. Use of Terms

For the purposes of this Convention:

"Biological diversity" means the variability among living organisms from all sources including *inter alia,* terrestrial, marine and other aquatic ecosystems and the ecological complexes of which they are part; this includes diversity within species, between species and of ecosystems.

"Biological resources" include genetic resources, organisms or parts thereof, populations, or any other biotic component of ecosystems with actual or potential use or value for humanity.

"Biotechnology" means any technological application that uses biological systems, living organisms, or derivatives thereof, to make or modify products or processes for specific use.

"Country of origin of genetic resources" means the country which possesses those genetic resources in in-situ coordination.

"Country providing genetic resources" means the country supplying genetic resources collected from in-situ sources, including populations of both wild and domesticated species, or taken from ex-situ sources, which may or may not have originated in that country.

"Domesticated or cultivated species" means species in which the evolutionary process has been influenced by humans to meet their needs.

"Ecosystem" means a dynamic complex of plant, animal and micro-organism communities and their non-living environment interacting as a functional unit.

"Ex-situ conservation" means the conservation of components of biological diversity outside their natural habitats.

"Genetic material" means any material of plant, animal microbial or other origin containing functional units of heredity.

"Genetic resources" means genetic material of actual or potential value.

"Habitat" means the place or type of site where an organism or population naturally occurs.

"In-situ conditions" means condition where genetic resources exist within ecosystems and natural habitats, and, in the case of domesticated or cultivated species, in the surroundings where they have developed their distinctive properties.

"In-situ conservation" means the conservation of ecosystems and natural habitats and the maintenance and recovery of viable populations of species in their natural surroundings and in the case of domesticated or cultivated species, in the surrounding where they have developed their distinctive properties.

"Regional economic integration organization" means an organization constituted by sovereign States of a given region, to which its member States have transferred competence in respect of matters governed by this Convention and which has been duly authorised, in accordance with its internal procedures, to sign, ratify, accept, approve or accede to it.

"Sustainable use" means the use of components of biological diversity in a way and at a rate that does not lead to the long term decline of biological diversity, thereby maintaining its potential to meet the need the aspirations of present and future generations.

"Technology" includes biotechnology.

Article 3. Principles

States have, in accordance with the Charter of the United Nations and the principles of international law, the sovereign right to expolit their own resources pursuant to their own environmental policies, and the responsibility to ensure that activities within their jurisdiction or control do not cause damage to the environment of other States or of areas beyond the limits of national jurisdiction.

Article 4. Jurisdictional Scope

Subject to the rights of other States, and except as otherwise expressly provided in this Convention, the provisions of this Convention apply, in relation to each Contracting Party:

(a) In the case of components of biological diversity, in areas within the limits of its national jurisdiction; and

(b) In the case of processes and activities, regardless of where their effects occur, carried out under its jurisdiction or control, within the area of its national jurisdiction or beyond the limits of national jurisdiction.

Article 5. Cooperation

Each Contracting Party shall, as far as possible and as appropriate, cooperate with other Contracting Parties directly or, where appropriate, through competent international organizations, in respect of areas beyond national jurisdiction and on other matters of mutual interest, for the conservation and sustainable use of biological diversity.

Article 6. General Measures for Conservation and Sustainable Use

Each Contracting party shall in accordance with its particular conditions and capabilities:

(a) Develop national strategies, plans or programmes for the conservation and sustainable use of biological diversity or adapt for this purpose existing strategies, plans or programmes which shall reflect, *inter alia*, the measures set out in this Convention relevant to the Contracting Party concerned; and

(b) Integrate, as for as possible and as appropriate, the conservation and sustainable use of biological diversity into relevant sectorial or cross-sectorial plans, programmes and policies.

Article 7. Identification and Monitoring

Each Contracting Party shall, as far as possible and as appropriate, in particular for the purposes of Articles 8 to 10:

(a) Identify components of biological diversity important for its conservation and sustainable use having regard to the indicative list of categories set down in Annex I;

(b) Monitor, through sampling and other techniques, the components of biological diversity identified pursuant to subparagraph (a) above, paying particular attention to those requiring urgent conservation measures and those which offer the greatest potential for sustainable use;

(c) Identify processes and categories of activities which have or are likely to have significant adverse impacts on the conservation and sustainable use of biological diversity, and monitor their effects through sampling and other techniques; and

(d) Maintain and organize, by any mechanism data devised from identification and monitoring activities pursuant to subparagraphs (a), (b) and (c) above.

Article 8. In-situ Conservation

Each Contracting Party shall, as far as possible and as appropriate:

(a) Establish a system of protected areas or areas where special measures need to be taken to conserve biological diversity;

(b) Develop, where necessary, guidelines for the selection, establishment and management of protected areas or areas where special measures need to be taken to conserve biological diversity;

(c) Regulate or manage biological resources important for the conservation of biological diversity whether within or outside protected areas, with a view to ensuring their conservation and sustainable use;

(d) Promote the protection of ecosystems, natural habitats and the maintenance of viable populations of species in natural surrounding;

(e) Promote environmentally sound and sustainable development in areas adjacent to protected areas with a view to furthering protection of these areas;

(f) Rehabilitate and restore degraded ecosystems and promote the recovery of threatened species, *inter alia,* through the development and implementation of plans or other management strategies;

(g) Establish or maintain means to regulate, manage or control the risks associated with the use and release of living modified organisms resulting from biotechnology which are likely to have adverse environmental impacts that could affect the conservation and sustainable use of biological diversity, taking also into account the risks to human health;

(h) Prevent the introduction of, control or eradicate those alien species which threaten ecosystems, habitats or species;

(i) Endeavour to provide the conditions needed for compatibility between present uses and the conservation of biological diversity and the sustainable use of its components;

(j) Subject to its national legislation, respect, preserve and maintain knowledge, innovations and practices of indigenous and local communities embodying traditional lifestyles relevant for the conservation and sustainable use of biological diversity and promote their wider application with the approval and involvement of the holders of such knowledge, innovations and practices and encourage the equitable sharing of the benefits arising from the utilization of such knowledge, innovations and practices;

(k) Develop or maintain necessary legislation and/or other regulatory provisions for the protection of threatened species and populations;

(l) Where a significant adverse effect on biological diversity has been determined pursuant to Article 7, regulate or manage the relevant processes and categories of activities; and

(m) Cooperate in providing financial and other support for in-situ conservation outlined in subparagraphs (a) to (1) above, particularly to developing countries.

Article 9. Ex-situ Conservation

Each Contracting Party shall, as far as possible and as appropriate, and predominantly for the purpose of complementing in-situ measures:

(a) Adopt measures for the ex-situ conservation of components of biological diversity, preferably in the country of origin of such components;

(b) Establish and maintain facilities for ex-situ conservation of and research on plants, animals and micro-organism, preferably in the country of origin of genetic resources;

(c) Adopt measures for the recovery and rehabilitation of threatened species and for their reintroduction into their natural habitats under appropriate conditions;

(d) Regulate and manage collection of biological resources from natural habitats for ex-situ conservation purposes so as not to threaten ecosystems and in-situ measures are required under subparagraph (c) above; and

(e) Cooperate in providing financial and other support for ex-situ conservation outlined in subparagraphs (a) to (d) above and in the establishment and maintenance of ex-situ conservation facilities in developing countries.

Article 10. Sustainable Use of Components of Biological Diversity

Each Contracting Party shall, as far as possible and as appropriate:

(a) Integrate consideration of the conservation and sustainable use of biological resources into national decision making;

(b) Adopt measures relating to the use of biological resources to avoid or minimize adverse impacts on biological diversity;

(c) Protect and encourge customary use of biological resources in accordance with traditional cultural practices that are compatible with conservation or sustainable use/requirements;

(d) Support local populations to develop and implement remedial action in degraded areas where biological diversity has been reduced; and

(e) Encourage cooperation between its governmental authorities and its private sector in developing methods for sustainable use of biological resources.

Article 11. Incentive Measures

Each Contracting party shall, as far as possible and as appropriate, adopt economically and socially sound measures that act as incentives for the conservation and sustainable use of components of biological diversity.

Article 12. Research and Training

The Contracting Parties, taking into account the special needs of developing countries, shall:

(a) Establish and maintain programmes for scientific and technical education and training in measures for the identification, conservation and sustainable use of biological diversity and its components and provide support for such education and training for the specific needs of developing countries;.

(b) Promote and encourage research which contributes to the conservation and sustainable use of biological diversity, particulary in developing countries, *inter alia*, in accordance with decisions of the Conference of the Parties taken in consequence of recommendations of the Subsidiary Body on Scientific, Technical and Technological Advice; and

(c) In keeping with the provisions of Articles 16, 18 and 20, promote and cooperate in the use of scientific advances in biological diversity research in develping methods for conservation and sustainable use of biological resources.

Article 13. Public Education and Awareness

The Contracting Parties shall:

(a) Promote and encourage understanding of the importance of, and the measures required for, the conservation of biological diversity, as well as its propagation through media, and the inclusion of these topics in educational programmes; and

(b) Cooperate, as appropriate, with other States, and international organizations in developing educational and public awareness programmes with respect to conservation and sustainable use of biological diversity.

Article 14. Impact Assessment and Minimizing Adverse Impacts

1. Each Contracing Party, as far as possible and as appropriate shall

(a) Introduce appropriate procedures requiring environmental impact assessment of its proposed projects that are likely to have significant adverse effects on biological diversity with a view to avoiding or minimizing such effects and, where appropriate, allow for public participation in such procedures;

(b) Introduce appropriate arrangements to ensure that the environmental consequences of its programmes and policies that are likely to have significant adverse impacts on biological diversity are duly taken into account;

(c) Promote, on the basis of reciprocity, notification, exchange of information and consultation on activities under their jurisdiction or control which are likely to significantly affect adversely the biologically diversity of other States or areas beyond the limits of national jurisdiction, by encouraging the conclusion of bilateral, regional or multilateral arrangements, as appropriate;

(d) In the case of imminent or grave danger or damage, originating under its jurisdiction or control, to biological diversity within the area under jurisdiction of other States or in areas beyond the limits of national jurisdiction, notify immediately the potentially affected States of such danger or damage, as well as initiate action to prevent or minimize such danger or damage; and

(e) Promote national arrangements for emergency responses to activities or events, whether caused naturally or otherwise, which present a grave and imminent danger to biological diversity and encourage international cooperation to supplement such national efforts and, where appropriate and agreed by the States or regional economic integration organizations concerned, to establish joint contingency plans.

2. The Conference of the Parties shall examine on the basis of studies to be carried out, the issue of liability and redress, including restoration and compensation, for damage to biological diversity, except where such liability is a purely internal matter.

Article 15. Access to Genetic Resources

1. Recognizing the sovereign rights of States over their natural resources, the authority to determine access to genetic resources rests with the national governments and is subject to national legislation.
2. Each Contracting Party shall endeavour to create conditions to facilitate access to genetic resources for environmentally sound uses by other Contracting Parties and not to impose restrictions that run counter to the objectives of this Convention.
3. For the purpose of this Convention, the genetic resources being provided by a Contracting Party, as referred to in this Article and Articles 16 and 19, are only those that are provided by Contracting Parties that are countries of origin of such resources or by the Parties that have acquired the genetic resources in accordance with this Convention.
4. Access, where granted, shall be on mutually agreed terms and subject to the provisions of this Artcle.
5. Access to genetic resources shall be subject to prior informed consent of the Contracting Party providing such resources, unless otherwise determined by that Party.
6. Each Contracting Party shall endeavour to develop and carry out scientific research base on genetic resources provided by other Contracting Parties with the full participation of, and where possible, in such Contracting Parties.
7. Each Contracting Party shall take legislative, administrative or policy measures, as appropriate, and

in accordance with Articles 16 and 19 and, where necessary through the financial mechanism established by Articles 20 and 21 with the aim of sharing in a fair and equitable way the results of research and developement and the benefit arising from the commercial and other utilization of genetic resources with the Contracting Party providing such resources. Such sharing shall be upon mutually agreed terms.

Article 16. Access to and Transfer of Technology

1. Each Contracting Party, recognizing that technology includes biotechnology, and that both access to and trnasfer of technology among Contractinfg Parties are essential elements for the attainment of the objective of this Convention, undertakes subject to the provisions of this Article to provide and/or facilitate access and transfer to other Contracting Parties of technologies that are relevant to the conservation and sustainable use of biological diversity or make use of genetic resources and do not cause significant damage to the environment.
2. Access to and transfer of technology referred to in paragraph 1 above to developing countries shall be provided and/or facilitated under fair and most favourable terms, including on concessional and preferential terms where mutually agreed, and, where necessary, in accordance with the financial mechanism established by Articles 20 and 21. In the case of technology subject to patents and other intellectual property rights, such access and transfer shall be provided on terms which recognize and are consistent with the adequate and effective protection of intellectual property rights. The application of this paragraph shall be consistent with paragraphs 3,4 and 5 below.
3. Each Contracting Party shall take legislative, administrative or policy measures, as appropriate, with

the aim that Contracting Parties, in particular those that are developing countries, which provide genetic resources are provided access to and transfer of technology which makes use of those resources, on mutually agreed terms including technology protected by patents and other intellectual property rights, where necessary, through the international law and consistent with paragraphs 4 and 5 below.

4. Each Contracting Party shall take legislative administrative or policy measures, as appropriate, with the aim that the private sector facilitates access to, joint development and transfer of technology referred to in paragraph 1 above for the benefit of both governmental institutions and the private sector of developing countries and in this regard shall abide by the obligations included in paraghaphs 1, 2 and 3 above.
5. The Contracting Parties, recognizing that patents and other intellectual property rights may have an influence on the implementation of this Convention, shall cooperate in this regard subject to national legislation and international law in order to ensure that such rights are supportive of and do not run counter to its objectives.

Article 17. Exchange of Information

1. The Contracting Parties shall facilitate the exchange of information, from all publicity available sources, relevant to the conservation and sustainable use of biological diversity, taking into account the special needs of developing countries.
2. Such exchange of information shall include exchange of results of technical, scientific and socio-economic research, as well as information on training and surveying programmes, specialized knowledge, indigenous and traditional knowledge as such and in combination with the technologies referred to in Article

16, paragraph 1. It shall also, where feasible, include repatriation of information.

Article 18. Technical and Scientific Cooperation

1. The Contracting Parties shall promote international technical and scientific cooperation in the field of conservation and sustainable use of biological diversity, where necessary, through the appropriate international and national institutions.
2. Each Contracting Party shall promote technical and scientific cooperation with other Contracting Parties, in particular developing countries, in implementing this Convention, *inter alia,* through the development and implementation of national policies. In promoting such cooperartion, special attention should be given to the development and strengthening of national capabilities, by means of human resources development and institution building.
3. The conference of the Parties, at its first meeting, shall determine how to establish a clearing-house mechanism to promote and facilitate technical and scientific cooperation.
4. The Contracting Parties shall, in accordance with national legislation and policies, encourage and develop methods of cooperation for the development and use of technologies, including indigenous and traditional technologies, in pursuance of the objectives of this Convention. For this purpose, the Contracting Parties shall also promote cooperation in the training of personnel and exchange experts.
5. The Contracting Parties shall subject to mutual agreement, promote the establishment of joint research programmes and joint ventures for the development of technologies relevant to the objectives of this Covention.

Article 19. Handling of Biotechnology and Distribution of its Benefits

1. Each Contracting party shall take legislative, administrative or policy measures, as appropriate, to provide for the effective participation in biotechnological research activities by those Contracting Parties, especially developing countries, which provide the genetic resources for such research, and where feasible, in such Contracting Parties.
2. Each Contracting Party shall take all practicable measures to promote and advance priority access on a fair and equitable basis by Contracting Parties, especially developing countries, to the results and benefits arising from biotechnologies based upon genetic resources provided by those Contracting Parties. Such access shall be on mutually agreed terms.
3. The Parties shall consider the need for and modalities of a protocol setting out appropriate procedures, including, in particular, advance informed agreement, in the field of the safe transfer, handling and use of any living modified organism resulting from biotechnology that may have adverse effect on the conservation and sustainable use of biological diversity.
4. Each Contracting Party shall, directly or by requiring any natural or legal person under its jurisdiction providing the organisms referred to in paragraph 3 above, provide any available information about the use and safety regulations required by that Contracting Party in handling such organisms, as well as any available information on the potential adverse impact of the specific organisms concerned to the Contracting Party into which those organisms are to be introduced.

Article 20. Financial Resources

1. Each Contracting Party undertakes to provide, ir

accordance with its capabilities, finanacial support and incentives in respect of those national activities which are intended to achieve the objectives of this Convention, in accordance with its national plans, priorities and programmes.

2. The developed country Parties shall provide new and additional financial resources to enable developing country Parties to meet the agreed full incremental costs to them of implementing measures which fulfil the obligations of this Convention and to benefit from its provisions and which costs are agreed between a developing country Party and the institutional structure referred to programme, priorities and eligibility criteria and an inference of the parties. Other Parties, including countries undergoing the process of transition to a market economy, may voluntarily assume the obligations of the developed country Parties. For the purpose of this Article, the Conference of the Parties, shall at its first meeting establish a list of developed country Parties and other Parties which voluntarily assume the obligations of the developed country Parties. The Conference of the Parties shall periodically review and if necessary, amend the list. Contributions from other countries and sources on a voluntary basis would also be encouraged. The implementation of these commitments shall take into account the need for adequacy, predictability and timely flow of funds and the importance of burden-sharing among the contributing Parties included in the list.
3. The developed country Parties may also provide, and developing country Parties avail themselves of financial resources related to the implementation of this Convention through bilateral, regional and other multilateral channels.

4. The extent to which developing country Parties will effectively implement their commitments under this Convention will depend on the effecitve implementation by developed country Parties of their commitments under this Convention related to financial resources and transfer of technology and will take fully into account the fact that economic and social development and eradication of poverty are the first and overriding priorities of the developing country Parties.
5. The Parties shall take full account of the specific needs and special situation of least developed countries in their actions with regard to funding and transfer of technology.
6. The Contracting Parties shall also take into consideration the special conditions resulting from the dependence on, distribution and location of, biologial diversity within developing country Parties, in particular, small islands States.
7. Consideration shall also be given to the special situation of developing countries, including those that are most environmentally vulnerable, such as those with arid and semi-arid zones, coastal and mountainous areas.

Article 21. Financial Mechanism

1. There shall be a mechanism for the provision of financial resources to developing country Parties for purposes of this Convention on a grant or concessional basis the essential elements of which are described in this Article. The mechanism shall function under the authority and guidance of, and be accountable to the Conference of the Parties for purposes of this Convention. The operations of the mechanism shall be carried out by such institutional structure as may be decided upon by the Conference of the Parties at its first meeting. For purposes of the Convention, the

Conference of the Parties shall determine the policy, strategy, programme priorities and eligibility criteria relating to the access to and utilization of such resources. The contributions shall be such as to take into account the need for predictability, adequacy and timely flow of funds referred to in Articel 20 in accordance with the amount of resources needed to be decided periodically by the Conference of the Parties and the importance of burden-sharing among the contributing Parties included in the list referred to in Article 20, paragraph 2. Voluntary contributions may also be made by the developed country Parties and by other countries and sources. The mechanism shall operate within a democratic and transparent system of governance.

2. Pursuant to the objectives of this Convention, the Conference of the Parties shall at its first meeting determine the policy, strategy and programme priorities, as well as detailed criteria and guidelines for eligibility for access to and utilization of the financial resources including monitoring and evaluation on a regular basis of such utilization. The Conference of the parties shall decide on the arrangements to give effect to paragraph 1 above after consultation with the institutional structure entrusted with the operation of the financial mechanism.
3. The Conference of the Parties shall review the effectiveness of the mechanism established under this Article, including the criteria and guidelines referred to in paragraph 2 above, not less than two years after the entry into force of this Convention and thereafter on a regular basis. Based on such review, it shall take appropriate action to improve the effectivness of the mechanism if necessary.
4. The Contracting Parties shall consider strengthening existing financial institutions to provided financial

resources for the conservation and sustainable use of biological diversity.

Article 22. Relationship with Other International Conventions

1. The provisions of this Convention shall not affect the rights and obligations of any Contracting Party deriving from any existing international agreement, except where the exercise of those rights and obligations would cause a serious damage or threat to biological diversity.
2. Contracting Parties shall implement this Convention with respect to the marine environment consistently with the rights and obligations of States under the law of the sea.

Artcle 23. Conference of the Parties

1. A Conference of the Parties is hereby established. The first meeting of the Conference of the Parties shall be convened by the Executive Director of the United Nations Environment Programme not later than one year after the entry into force of this Convention. Thereafter, ordinary meetings of the Conference of the Parties shall be held at regular intervals to be determined by the Conference at its first meeting.
2. Extraordinary meetings of the Conference of the Parties shall be held at such other times as may be deemed necessary by the Conference, or at the written request of any Party, provided that, within six months of the request being communicated to them by the Secretariat, it is supported by at least one third of the Parties.
3. The Conference of the Parties shall by consensus agree upon and adopt rules of procedure for itself and for any subsidiary body it may establish, as well as financial rules governing the funding of the Secretariat. At each

ordinary meeting, it shall adopt a budget for the financial period until the next ordinary meeting.

4. The Conference of the Parties shall keep under review the implementation of this Convention, and, for this purpose, shall:
   (a) Establish the form and the intervals for transmitting the information to be submitted in accordance with Article 26 and consider such information as well as reports submitted by any subsidary body;
   (b) Review scientific, technical and technological advice on biological diversity provided in accordance with Article 25;
   (c) Consider and adopt, as required, protocols in accordance with Article 28;
   (d) Consider and adopt, as required, in accordance with Articles 29 and 30, amendments to this Convention and its annexes;
   (e) Consider amendments to any protocol, as well as to any annexes thereto, and, if so decided, recommend their adoption to the parties to the protocol concerned;
   (f) Consider and adopt, as required, in accordance with Article 30, additional annexes to this Convention;
   (g) Establish such subsidiary bodies, particularly to provide scientific and technical advice, as are deemed necessary for the implementation of this Convention;
   (h) Contact, through the secretariat, the executive bodies of conventions dealing with matters covered by this Convention with a view to establishing appropriate forms of cooperation with them; and
   (i) Consider and undertake any additional action that may be required for the achievement of the purposes of this Convention in the light of experience gained in its operation.

5. The United Nations, its specialized agencies and the

International Atomic Energy Agency, as well as any State not Party to this Convention, may be represented as observers at meetings of the Conference of the Parties. Any other body or agency, whether governmental, or non-governmental, qualified in fields relating to conservation and sustainable use of biological diversity, which has informed the Secretariat of its wish to be represented as an observer at a meeting of the Conference of the Parties, may be admitted unless at least one third of the Parties present object. The admission and participation of observers shall be subject to the rules of procedure adopted by the Conference of the Parties.

Article 24. Secretariat

1. A secretariat is hereby established. Its functions shal be:
   (a) To arrange for and service meetings of the Conference of the Parties provided for in Article 23;
   (b) To perform the functions assigned to it by any protocol;
   (c) To prepare reports on the execution of its functions under this Convention and present them to the Conference of the Parties;
   (d) To coordinate with other relevant international bodies and, in particular to enter into such administrative and contractual arrangements as may be required for the effective discharge of its functions; and
   (e) To perform such other functions as may be determined by the Conference of the Parties.
2. At its first ordinary meeting, the Conference of the Parties shall designate the secretariat from amongst those existing competent international organizations which have signified their willingness to carry out the secretariat functions under this Convention.

Article 25. Subsidiary Body on Scientific, Technical and Technological Advice

1. A subsidiary body for the provision of scientific, technical and technological advice is hereby established to provide the Conference of the Parties and, as appropriate, its other subsidiary bodies with timely advice relating to the implementation of this Convention. This body shall be open to participation by all Parties and shall be multidisciplinary. It shall comprise government representatives competent in the relevent field of expertise. It shall report regularly to the Conference of the Parties on all aspects of its work.
2. Under the authority of and in accordance with guidelines laid down by the Conference of the Parties, and upon its request, this body shall:
   (a) Provide scientific and technical assessments of the status of biological diversity;
   (b) Prepare scientific and technical assessments of the effects of types of measures taken in accordance with the provisions of this Convention;
   (c) Identify innovative, efficient and state-of-the-art technologies and know-how relating to the conservation and sustainable use of biological diversity and advise on the ways and means of promoting development and/or transferring such technologies;
   (d) Provide advice on scientific programmes and international cooperation in research and development related to conservation and sustainable use of biological diversity; and
   (e) Respond to scientific, technical, technological and methodological questions that the Conference of the Parties and its subsidiary bodies may put to the body.

3. The functions, terms of reference, organization and operation of this body may be further elaborated by the Conference of the Parties.

Article 26. Reports

Each Contracting Party shall, at intervals to be determined by the Conference of the Parties, present to the Conference reports of the implementation of the provisions of this Convention and their effectiveness in meeting the objectives of this Convention.

Article 27. Settlement of Disputes

1. In the event of a dispute between Contracting Parties concerning the interpretation or application of this Convention, the parties concerned shall seek solution by negotiation.
2. If the parties concerned cannot reach agreement by negotiation, they may jointly seek the good offices of, or request mediation by, a third party.
3. When ratifying, accepting, approving or acceding to this Convention, or at any time thereafter, a State or regional economic integration organization may declare in writing to the Depositary that for a dispute not resolved in accordance with paragraph 1 or paragraph 2 above, it accepts one or both of the following means of dispute settlement as compulsory:
   (a) Arbitration in accordance with the procedure laid down in Part 1 of Annex II;
   (b) Submission of the dispute to the International Court of Justice.
4. If the parties to the dispute have not, in accordance with paragrah 3 above, accepted the same or any procedure, the dispute shall be submitted to conciliation in accordance with Part 2 of Annex II unless the parties otherwise agree.

5. The provisions of this Article shall apply with respect to any protocol except as otherwise provided in the protocol concerned.

Article 28. Adoption of Protocols

1. The contracting Parties shall cooperate in the formulation and adoption of protocols to this Convention.
2. Protocols shall be adopted at a meeting of the Conference of the Parties.
3. The text of any proposed protocol shall be communicated to the Contracting Parties by the Secretariat at least six months before such a meeting.

Article 29. Amendment of the Convention or Protocols

1. Amendments to this Convention may be proposed by any Contracting Party. Amendments to any protocol may be proposed by any Party to that protocol.
2. Amendments to this Convention shall be adopted at a meeting of the Conference of the Parties. Amendments to any protocol shall be adopted at a meeting of the parties to the Protocol in question. The text of any proposed amendment to this Convention or, to any protocol, except as may otherwise be provided in such protocol, shall be communicated to the Parties to the instrument in question by the secretariat at least six months before the meeting at which it is proposed for adoption. The secretariat shall also communicate proposed amendments to the signatories to this Convention for information.
3. The Parties shall make every effort to reach agreement on any proposed amendment to this convention or to any protocol by consensus. If all efforts at consensus have been exhausted, and no agreement is reached, the amendment shall as a last resort be adopted by a two-

thirds majority vote of the Parties to the instrument in question present and voting at the meeting, and shall be submitted by the Depositary to all Parties for ratification, acceptance or approval.

4. Ratification, acceptance or approval of amendments shall be notified to the Depositary in writing. Amendments adopted in accordance with paragraph 3 above shall enter into force among Parties having accepted them on the ninetieth day after the deposit of instruments of ratification, acceptance or approval by at least two-thirds of the Contracting Parties to this Convention or of the Parties to the protocol concerned, except as may otherwise be provided in such protocol. Thereafter the amendments shall enter into force for any other Party on the ninetieth day after that Party deposits its instruments of ratification, acceptance or approval of the amendments.
5. For the purposes of this Article, "Parties present and voting" means Parties present and casting an affirmative or negative vote.

Article 30. Adoption and Amendment of Annexes

1. The annexes to this Convention or to any protocol shall form an integral part of the Convention or of such protocol, as the case may be and unless expressly provided otherwise, a reference to this Convention or its protocols constitutes at the time a reference to any annexes thereto. Such annexes shall be restricted to procedural, scientific, technical and administrative matters.
2. Except as may be otherwise provided in any protocol with respect to its annexes, the following procedure shall apply to the proposal, adoption and entry into force of additional annexes to this Convention or of annexes to any protocol:

   (a) Annexes to this Convention or to any protocol shall

be proposed and adopted according to the procedure laid down in Article 29;

(b) Any Party that is unable to approve an additional annex to this Convention or an annex to any protocol to which it is Party shall so notify the Depositary, in writing, within one year from the date of the communication of the adoption by the Depositary. The Depositary shall without delay notify all Parties of any such notification received. A Party may at any time withdraw a previous declaration of objection and the annexes shall therupon enter into force for that Party subject to subparagraph (c) below;

(c) On the expiry of one year from the date of the communication of the adoption by the Depositary, the annex shall enter into force for all Parties to this Convention or to any protocol concerned which have not submitted a notification in accordance with the provisions of subparagraph (b) above.

3. The proposal, adoption and entry into force of amendments to annexes to this Convention or to any protocol, the additional annex or amendment shall not enter into force until such time as the amendment to the Convention or to the protocol concerned enters into force.

4. If an additional annex or an amendment to an annex is related to an amendment to this Convention or to any protocol, the additional annex or amendment shall not enter into force until such time as the amendment to the Convention or to the protocol concerned enters into force.

Article 31. Right to Vote

1. Except as provided for in paragraph 2 below, each Contracting Party to this Convention or to any protocol shall have one vote.
2. Regional economic integration organizations, in matters

within their competence, shall exercise their right to vote with a number of votes equal to the number of their member States which are Contracing Parties to this Convention or the relevant protocol. Such organizations shall not exercise their right to vote if their member States exercise theirs, and vice versa.

Article 32. Relationship between this Convention and its Protocols

1. A State or a regional economic integration organization may not become a Party to protocol unless it is, or becomes at the same time, a Contracting Party to this Convention.
2. Decisions under any protocol shall be taken only by the Parties to the protocol concerned. Any Contracting Party that has not ratified, accepted or approved a protocol may participate as an observer in any meeting or the parties to that protocol.

Article 33. Signature

This Convention shall be open for signature at Rio de Janerio by all States and any regional economic integration organization from 5 June 1992 until 14 June 1992, and at the United Nations headquarters in New York from 15 June 1992 to 4 June 1993.

Article 34. Ratification, Acceptance or Approval

1. This Convention and any protocol shall be subject to ratification, acceptance or approval by States and by regional economic integration organizations. Instruments of ratification, acceptance or approval shall be deposited with the depositary.
2. Any organization referred to in paragraph 1 above which becomes a Contracting Party to this Convention or any protocol without any of its member States being a Contracting Party shall be bound by all the obligations

under the Convention or the protocol, as the case may be. In the case of such organization, one or more of whose member States is a Contracting Party to this Convention or relevant protocol, the organization and its member States shall decide on their respective responsibilities for the performance of their obligations under the Convention or protocol, as the case may be. In such cases, the organization and the member States shall not be entitled to exercise rights under the Convention or relevant protocol concurrently.

3. In their instruments of ratification, acceptance or approval, the organizations referred to in paragraph 1 above shall declare the extent of their competence with respect to the matters governed by the Convention or the relevant protocol. These organizations shall also inform the Depositary of any relevant modification in the extent of their competence.

Article 35. Accession

1. This Convention and any protocol shall be open for accession by States and by regional economic integration organization from the date on which the Convention or the protocol concerned is closed for signature. The instruments of accession shall be deposited with the Depositary.
2. In their instruments of accession, the organizations referred to in paragraph 1 above shall declare the extent of their competence with respect to the matters governed by the Convention or the relevant protocol. These organizations shall also inform the Depositary of any relevant modification in the extent of their competence.
3. The provision of Article 34, paragraph 2, shall apply to regional economic integration organizations which accede to this Convention or any protocol.

Article 36. Entry into Force

1. This Convention shall enter into force on the ninetieth day after the date of deposit of the thirtieth instrument of ratification, acceptance, approval or accession.
2. Any protocol shall enter into force on the ninetieth day after the date of deposit of the number of instruments of ratification, acceptance, approval or accession, specified in that protocol, has been deposited.
3. For each Contracting Party which ratifies, accepts or approves this Convention or accedes thereto after the deposit of the thirtieth instrument of ratification, acceptance, approval or accession, it shall enter into force on the ninetieth day after the date of deposit by such Contracting Party of its instrument of ratification, acceptance, approval or accession.
4. Any protocol, except as otherwise provided in such protocol, shall enter into force for a Contracting Party that ratifies, accepts or approves that protocol or accedes thereto after its entry into force pursuant to paragraph 2 above, on the ninetieth day after the date on which that Contracting Party deposits its instrument of ratification, acceptance, approval or accession, or on the date on which this Convention enters into force for that Contracting Party, whichever shall be the later.
5. For the purposes of paragraph 1 and 2 above, any instrument deposited by a regional economic integration organization shall not be counted as additional to those deposited by member State of such organization.

Article 37. Reservations

No reservations may be made to this Convention.

Article 38. Withdrawls

1. At any time after two years from the date on which this Convention has entered into force for a Contracting

Party, that Contracting Party may withdraw after the date of deposit of the thirtieth instrument of ratification, acceptance, approval or accession.

3. Any Contracting Party which withdraws from this Convention shall be considered as also having withdrawn from any protocol to which it is party.

Article 39. Financial Interim Arrangements

Provided that it has been fully restructured in accordance with the requirements of Article 21, the Global Environmental facility of the United Nations Development Programme, the United Nations Environment Programme and the International Bank for Reconstruction and Development shall be the institutional structure referred to in Article 21 on an interim basis, for the period between the entry into force of this Convention and the first meeting of the Conference of the Parties or until the Conference of the Parties decides which institutional structure will be designated in accordance with Article 21.

Article 40. Secretariat Interim Arrangements

The secretariat to be provided by the Executive Director of the United Nations Environment Programme shall be the secretariat referred to in Article 24, paragraph 2, on an interim basis for the period between the entry into force of this Convention and the first meeting of the Conference of the Parties.

Article 41. Depositary

The Secretary General of the United Nations shall assume the functions of Depositary of this Convention and any protocols.

Article 42. Authentic Texts

The original of the Convention, of which the Arabic, Chinese,

English, French, Russian and Spanish texts are equally authentic, shall be deposited with the Secretary General of the United Nations.

In witness whereof the undersigned, being duly authorized to that effect, have signed this Convention.

Done at Rio de Janeiro on this fifth day of June, one thousand nine hundred and ninety two.

ANNEX I

IDENTIFICATION AND MONITORING

1. Ecosystems and habitats: containing high diversity, large numbers of endemic or threatened species, or wilderness; required by migratory species; of social, economic, cultural or scientific importance; or, which are representative, unique or associated with key evolutionary or other biological processes;
2. Species and communities which are: threatened; wild relatives of domesticated or cultivated species; of medicinal, agricultural or other economic value; or social, scientific or cultural importance; or importance for research into the conservation and sustainable use of biological diversity, such as indicatory species; and
3. Described genomes and genes of social, scientific or economic importance.

ANNEX II
(Part I)

ARBITRATION

Article 1

The claimant party shall notify the secretariat that the parties are referring a dispute to arbitration pursuant to Article 27

The notification shall state the subject matter of arbitration and include, in particular, the articles of the Convention or the protocol, the interpretation or application of which are at issue. If the parties do not agree on the subject matter of the dispute before the President of the tribunal as designated, the arbitral tribunal shall determine the subject matter. The secretariat shall forward the information thus received to all Contracting Parties to this Convention or to the protocal concerned.

Article 2

1. In disputes between two parties, the arbitral tribunal shall consist of three members. Each of the parties to the dispute shall appoint an arbitrator and the two arbitrators so appointed shall designate by common agreement the third arbitrator who shall be the President of the tribunal. The later shall not be national of one of the parties to the dispute, nor have his or her usual place of residence in the territory of one of these parties, nor be employed by any of them nor have dealt with the case in any other capacity.
2. In disputes between more than two parties, parties in the same interest shall appoint one arbitrator jointly by agreement.
3. Any vacancy shall be filled in the manner prescribed for the initial appointment.

Article 3

1. If the President of the arbitral tribunal has not been designated within two months of the appointment of the second arbitrator, the Secretary General of the United Nations shall, at the request of a party, designate the President within a further two month period.
2. If one of the parties to the dispute does not appoint an arbitrator within two months of receipt of the request,

the other party may inform the Secretary General who shall make the designation within a further two-month period.

Article 4

The arbitral tribunal shall render its decisions in accordance with the provisions of the Convention, any protocols concerned, and international law.

Article 5

Unless the parties to the dispute otherwise agree, the arbitral tribunal shall determine its own rules of procedure.

Article 6

The arbitral tribunal may, at the request of one of the parties, recommend essential interim measures of protection.

Article 7

The parties to the dispute shall facilitate the work of the arbitral tribunal and, in particular, using all means at their disposal, shall:

(a) Provide it with all relevant documents, information and facilities; and
(b) Enable it, when necessary, to call withesses or experts and receive their evidence.

Article 8

The parties and the arbitrators are under an obligation to protect the confidentiality of any information they receive in confidence during the proceeding of the arbitral tribunal.

Article 9

Unless the arbitral tribunal determines otherwise because of the particular circumstances of the case, the costs of the tribunal shall be borne by the parties to the dispute in equal shares. The tribunal shall keep a record of all its costs, and shall furnish a final statement thereof to the parties.

Article 10

Any Contracting Party that has an interest of a legal nature in the subject matter of the dispute which may be affected by the decision in the case, may intervene in the proceedings with the consent of the tribunal.

Article 11

The tribunal may hear and determine counter claims arising directly out of the subject matter of the dispute.

Article 12

Decisions both on procedure and substance of the arbitral tribunal shall be taken by majority vote of its members.

Article 13

If one of the parties to the dispute does not appear before the arbitral tribunal or fails to defend its case, the other party may request the tribunal to continue the proceedings and to make its award. Absence of a party or a failure of a party to defend its case shall not constitute a bar to the proceedings. Before rendering its final decision, the arbitral tribunal must satisfy itself that the claim is well founded in fact and law.

Article 14

The tribunal shall render its final decision within five months of the date on which it is fully constituted unless it finds it necessary to extend the time limit for a period which should not exceed five more months.

Article 15

The final decision of the arbitral tribunal shall be confined to the subject matter of the dispute and shall state the reasons on which it is based. It shall contain the names of the members who have participated and the date of the final decision. Any member of the tribunal may attach a separate or dissenting opinion to the final decision.

Article 16

The award shall be binding on the parties to the dispute. It shall be without appeal unless the parties to the dispute have agreed in advance to an appellate procedure.

Article 17

Any controversy which may arise between the parties to the dispute as regards the interpretation or manner of implementation of the final decision may be submitted by either party for decision to the arbitral trbunal which rendered it.

Part II

CONCILIATION

Article 1

A conciliation commission shall be created upon the request of one of the parties to the dispute. The commission shall, unless the parties otherwise agree, be composed of five members, two appointed by each Party concerned and a President chosen jointly by those members.

Article 2

In disputes between more than two parties, parties in the same interest shall appoint their members of the commission jointly by agreement. Where two or more parties have separate interests or there is a disagreement as to whether they are of the same interest, they shall appoint their members separately.

Article 3

If any appointments by the parties are not made within two months of the date of the request to create a conciliation commissioin, the Secretary-General of the United Nations shall, if asked to do so by the party that made the request, make those appointments within a further two-month period.

Article 4

If a President of the conciliation commission has not been chosen within two months of the last of the members of the commission being appointed, the Secretary General of the United Nations shall, if asked to do so by a party, designate a President within a further two-month period.

Article 5

The conciliation commission shall take its decisions by majority vote of its members. It shall, unless the parties to the dispute otherwise agree, determine its own procedure. It shall render a proposal for resolution of the dipsute which the parties shall consider in good faith.

Article 6

A disagreement as to whether the conciliation commission has competence shall be decided by the commission.

APPENDIX III

Rio Declaration and Forest Principles

RIO DECLARATION ON ENVIRONMENT AND DEVELOPMENT

The United Nations Conference on Environment and Development,

Having met at Rio de Janeiro from 3 to 14 June, 1992,

Reaffirming the Declaration of the United Nations Conference on the Human Environment, adopted at Stockholm on 16 June, 1972, and seeking to build upon it,

With the goal of establishing a new and equitable global partnership through the creation of new levels of cooperation among States, key sectors of societies and people,

Working towards international agreements which respect the interests of all and protect the integrity of the global environmental and developmental system,

Recognizing the integral and interdependent nature of the Earth, our home,

Proclaims that:

Principle 1

Human beings are at the centre of concerns for sustainable development. They are entitled to a healthy and productive life in harmony with nature.

Principle 2

States have, in accordance with the Charter of the United Nations and the principles of international law, the sovereign right to exploit their own resources pursuant to their own environmental and developmental policies, and the responsibility to ensure that activities within their jurisdiction or control do not cause damage to the environment of other States or of areas beyond the limits of national jurisdiction.

Principle 3

The right to development must be fulfilled so as to equitably meet developmental and environmental needs of present and future generations.

Principle 4

In order to achieve sustainable development, environmental protection shall constitute an integral part of the development process and cannot be considered in isolation from it.

Principle 5

All States and all people shall cooperate in the essential task of eradicating poverty as an indispensable requirement for sustainable development, in order to decrease the disparities in standards of living and better meet the needs of the majority of the people of the world.

Principle 6

The special situation and needs of developing countries, particularly the least developed and those most environmentally vulnerable, shall be given special priority. International actions in the field of environmental and development should also address the interests and needs of all countries.

Principle 7

States shall cooperate in a spirit of global partnership to conserve, protect and restore the health and integrity of the Earth's ecosystem. In view of the different contributions to global environmental degradation, States have common but differentiated responsibilities. The developed countries acknowledge the responsibility that they bear in the international pursuit of sustainable development in view of the pressures their societies place on the global environment and of the technologies and financial resources they command.

Principle 8

To achieve sustainable development and a higher quality of life for all people, States should reduce and eliminate unsustainable patterns of production and consumption and promote appropriate demographic policies.

Principle 9

States should cooperate to strengthen endogenous capacity-building for sustainable development by improving scientific understanding through exchange of scientific and technological knowledge, and by enhancing the development, adaptation, diffusion and transfer of technologies, including new and innovative technologies.

Principle 10

Environmental issues are best handled with the participation of all concerned citizens, at the relevant level. At the national level, each individual shall have appropriate access to information concerning the environment that is held by public authorities, including information on hazardous materials and activities in their communities, and the opportunity to participate in decision-making processes. States shall facilitate and encourage public awareness and participation by making information widely available. Effective access to judicial and administrative proceedings, including redress and remedy, shall be provided.

Principle 11

States shall enact effective environmental legislation.

Environmental standards, management objectives and priorities should reflect the environmental and developmental context to which they apply. Standards applied by some countries may be inappropriate and of unwarranted economic and social cost to other countries, in particular developing countries.

Principle 12

States should cooperate to promote a supportive and open international economic system that would lead to economic growth and sustainable development in all countries, to better address the problems of environmental degradation. Trade policy measures for environmental purposes should not constitute a means of arbitrary or unjustifiable discrimination or a disguised restriction on international trade. Unilateral actions to deal with environmental challenges outside the jurisdiction of the importing country should be avoided. Environmental measures addressing transboundary or global environmental problems should, as far as possible, be passed on an international consensus.

Principle 13

States shall develop national law regarding liability and compensation for the victims of pollution and other environmental damage. States shall also cooperate in an expeditious and more determined manner to develop further international law regarding liability and compensation for adverse effects of environmental damage caused by activities within their jurisdiction or control to areas beyond their jurisdiction.

Principle 14

States should effectively cooperate to discourage or prevent the relocation and transfer to other States of any activities and substances that cause severe environmental degradation or are found to be harmful to human health.

Principle 15

In order to protect the environment, the precautionary approach shall be widely applied by States according to their capabilities. Where there are threats of serious or irreversible damage, lack of full scientific certainty shall not be used as a reason for postponing cost-effective measures to prevent environmental degradation.

Principle 16

National authorities should endeavour to promote the internalization of environmental costs and the use of economic instruments, taking into account the approach that the polluter should, in principle, bear the cost of pollution, with due regard to the public interest and without distorting international trade and investment.

Principle 17

Environmental impact assessment, as a national instrument, shall be undertaken for proposed activities that are likely to have a significant adverse impact on the environment and are subject to a decision of a competent national authority.

Principle 18

States shall immediately notify other States of any natural disasters or other emergencies that are likely to produce sudden harmful effects on the environment of those States. Every effort shall be made by the international community to help States so afflicted.

Principle 19

States shall provide prior and timely notification and relevant information to potentially affected States on activities that may have a significant adverse transboundary environmental effect and shall consult with those States at an early stage and in good faith.

Principle 20

Women have a vital role in environmental management and development. Their full participation is therefore essential to achieve sustainable development.

Principle 21

The creativity, ideals and courage of the youth of the world should be mobilized to forge a global partnership in order to achieve sustainable development and ensure a better future for all.

Principle 22

Indigenous people and their communities and other local communities have a vital role in environmental management and development because of their knowledge and traditional practices. States should recognize and duly support their identity, culture and interests and enable their effective participation in the achievement of sustainable development.

Principle 23

The environment and natural resources of people under oppression, domination and occupation shall be protected.

Principle 24

Warfare is inherently destructive of sustainable development. States shall therefore respect international law providing protection for the environment in times of armed conflict and cooperate in its further development, as necessary.

Principle 25

Peace, development and environmental protection are interdependent and indivisible.

Principle 26

States shall resolve all their environmental disputes peacefully and by appropriate means in accordance with the Charter of the United Nations.

Principle 27

States and people shall cooperate in good faith and in a spirit of partnership in the fulfilment of the principle embodied in this Declaration and in the further development of international law in the field of sustainable development.

NON-LEGALLY BINDING AUTHORITATIVE STATEMENT OF PRINCIPLES FOR A GLOBAL CONSENSUS ON THE MANAGEMENT, CONSERVATION AND SUSTAINABLE DEVELOPMENT OF ALL TYPES OF FORESTS

Preamble

(a) The subject of forests is related to the entire range of environmental and development issues and opportunities, including the right to socio-economic development on a sustainable basis.

(b) The guiding objective of these principles is to contribute to the management, conservation and sustainable development of forests and to provide for their multiple and complementary functions and uses.

(c) Forestry issues and opportunities should be examined in a holistic and balanced manner within the overall context of environment and development, taking into consideration the multiple functions and uses of forests, including traditional uses, and the likely economic and social stress when these uses are constrained or restricted, as well as potential for development that sustainable forest management can offer.

(d) These principles reflect a first global consensus on forests. In committing themselves to the prompt implementation of these principles, countries also decide to keep them under assessment for their adequacy with regard to further international cooperation on forest issues.

(e) These principles should apply to all types of forests, both natural and planted, in all geographical regions and climatic zones, including austral, boreal, subtemperate, temperate, subtropical and tropical.

(f) All types of forests embody complex and unique ecological processes which are the basis for their present and potential capacity to provide resources to satisfy human needs as well as environmental values, and as such their sound management and conservation is of concern to the Governments of the countries to which they belong and are of value to local communities and to the environment as a whole.

(g) Forests are essential to economic development and the maintenance of all forms of life.

(h) Recognizing that the responsibility for forest management, conservation and sustainable development is in many States allocated among federal/national, state/provincial and local levels of government, each State, in accordance with its constitution and/or national legislation, should pursue these principles at the appropriate level of government.

Principles/Elements

1. (a) States have, in accordance with the Charter of the

United Nations and the principles of international law, the sovereign right to exploit their own resources pursuant to their own environmental politics and have the responsibility to ensure that activities within their jurisdiction or control do not cause damage to the environment of other States or of areas beyond the limits of national jurisdiction.

(b) Forest resources and forest lands should be sustainably managed to meet the social, economic, ecological, cultural and spiritual needs of present and future generations. These needs are for forest products and services, such as wood and wood products, water, food, fodder, medicine, fuel, shelter, employment, recreation, habitats for wildlife, landscape diversity, carbon sinks and reservoirs, and for other forest products. Appropriate measures should be taken to protect forests against harmful effects of pollution, including air-borne pollution, fires, pests and diseases, in order to maintain their full multiple value.

(c) The provision of timely, reliable and accurate information on forests and forest ecosystems is essential for public understanding and informed decision-making and should be ensured.

(d) Governments should promote and provide opportunities for the participation of interested parties, including local communities and indigenous people, industries, labour, non-governmental organizations and individuals, forest dwellers and women, in the development, implementation and planning of national forest policies.

3. (a) National policies and strategies should provide a framework for increased efforts, including the development and strengthening of institutions and programmes for the management, conservation and sustainable development of forests and forest lands.

(b) International institutional arrangements, building on those organizations and mechanisms already in existence, as appropriate, should facilitate international cooperation in the field of forests.

(c) All aspects of environmental protection and social and economic development as they relate to forests and forest lands should be integrated and comprehensive.

4. The vital role of all types of forests in maintaining the ecological processes and balance at the local, national, regional and global levels through, *inter alia*, their role in protecting fragile ecosystems, watersheds and freshwater resources and as rich storehouse of biodiversity and biological resources and sources of genetic material for biotechnology products, as well as photosynthesis, should be recognized.

5. (a) National forest policies should recognize and duly support the identity, culture and the rights of indigenous people, their communities and other communities and forest dwellers. Appropriate conditions should be promoted for these groups to enable them to have an economic stake in forest use, perform economic activities, and achieve and maintain cultural identity and social organization, as well as adequate levels of livelihood and well-being, through, *inter alia*, those land tenure arrangements which serve as incentives for the sustainable management of forests.

(b) The full participation of women in all aspects of the management, conservation and sustainable development of forests should be actively promoted.

6. (a) All types of forests play an important role in meeting energy requirements through the provision of a renewable source of bio-energy, particularly in developing countries, and the demands for

fuelwood for household and industrial needs should be met through sustainable forest management, afforestation and reforestation. To this end, the potential contribution of plantation of both indigenous and introduced species for the provision of both fuel and industrial wood should be recognized.

(b) National policies and programmes should take into account the relationship, where it exists, between the conservation, management and sustainable development of forests and all aspects related to the production, consumption, recycling and/or final disposal of forest products.

(c) Decisions taken on the management, conservation and sustainable development of forest resources should benefit, to the extent practicable, from a comprehensive assessment of economic and non-economic values of forest good and services and of the environmental costs and benefits. The development and improvement of methodologies for such evaluations should be promoted.

(d) The role of planted forests and permanent agricultural crops as sustainable and environmentally sound sources of renewable energy and industrial raw material should be recognized, enhanced and promoted. Their contribution to the maintenance of ecological processes, to offsetting pressure on primary/old-growth forest and to providing regional employment and development with the adequate involvement of local inhabitants should be recognized and enhanced.

(e) Natural forests also constitute a source of goods and services, and their conservation, sustainable management and use should be promoted.

7. (a) Efforts should be made to promote a supportive international economic climate conducive to

sustained and environmentally sound development of forests in all countries, which include, *inter alia*, the promotion of sustainable patterns of production and consumption, the eradication of poverty and the promotion of food security.

(b) Specific financial resources should be provided to developing countries with significant forest areas which establish programmes for the conservation of forests including protected natural forest areas. These resources should be directed notably to economic sectors which would stimulate economic and social substitution activities.

8. (a) Efforts to maintain and increase forest cover and forest productivity should be undertaken in ecologically, economically and socially sound ways through the rehabilitation, reforestation and re-establishment of trees and forests on unproductive, degraded and deforested lands, as well as through the management of existing forest resources.

(c) The implementation of national policies and programmes aimed at forest management, conservation and sustainable development, particularly in developing countries, should be supported by international financial and technical cooperation, including through the private sector, where appropriate.

(d) Sustainable forest management and use should be carried out in accordance with national development policies and priorities and on the basis of environmentally sound national guidelines. In the formulation of such guidelines, account should be taken, as appropriate and if applicable, of relevant internationally agreed methodologies and criteria.

(e) Forest management should be integrated with management of adjacent areas so as to maintain ecological balance and sustainable productivity.

(f) National policies and/or legislation aimed at management, conservation and sustainable development of forests should include the protection of ecologically viable representative or unique examples of forests, including primary/old-growth forests, cultural, spiritual, historical, religious and other unique and valued forests of national importance.

(g) Access to biological resources, including genetic material, shall be with due regard to the sovereign rights of the countries where the forests are located and to the sharing on mutually agreed terms of technology and profits from biotechnology products that are derived from these resources.

(h) National policies should ensure that environmental impact assessments should be carried out where actions are likely to have significant adverse impacts on important forest resources, and where such actions are subject to a decision of a competent national authority.

9. (a) The efforts of developing countries to strengthen the management, conservation and sustainable development of their forest resources should be supported by the international community, taking into account the importance of redressing external indebtedness, particularly where aggravated by the net transfer of resources to developed countries, as well as the problem of achieving at least the replacement value of forests through improved market access for forest products, especially processed products. In this respect, special attention should also be given to the countries undergoing the process of transition to market economies.

(b) The problems that hinder efforts to attain the conservation and sustainable use of forest resources and that stem from the lack of alternative options available to local communities, in particular the urban poor and poor rural populations who are economically and socially dependent on forests and forest resources, should be addressed by Governments and the international community.

(c) National policy formulation with respect to all types of forests should take account of the pressures and demands imposed on forest ecosystems and resources from influencing factors outside the forest sector, and intersectoral means of dealing with these pressures and demands should be sought.

10. New and additional financial resources should be provided to developing countries to enable them to sustainably manage, conserve and develop their forest resources, including through afforestation, reforestation and combating deforestation and forest and land degradation.

11. In order to enable, in particular, developing countries to enhance their endogenous capacity and to better manage, conserve and develop their forest resources, the access to and transfer of environmentally sound technologies and corresponding know-how on favourable terms, including on concessional and preferential terms, as mutually agreed, in accordance with the relevant provisions of Agenda 21, should be promoted, facilitated and financed, as appropriate.

12. (a) Scientific research, forest inventories and assessments carried out by national institutions which take into account, where relevant, biological. physical, social and economic variables, as well as technological development and its application in the field of sustainable forest management, conservation and development, should be strengthened through effective modalities, including international cooperation. In this context, attention should also be given to

research and development of sustainably harvested non-wood products.

(b) National and, where appropriate, regional and international institutional capabilities in education, training, science, technology, economics, anthropology and social aspects of forests and forest management are essential to the conservation and sustainable development of forests and should be strengthened.

(c) International exchange of information on the results of forest and forest management research and development should be enhanced and broadened, as appropriate, making full use of education and training institutions, including those in the private sector.

(d) Appropriate indigenous capacity and local knowledge regarding the conservation and sustainable development of forests should, through institutional and financial support and in collaboration with the people in the local communities concerned, be recognized, respected, recorded, developed and, as appropriate, introduced in the implementation of programmes. Benefits arising from the utilization of indigenous knowledge should therefore be equitably shared with such people.

13. (a) Trade in forest products should be based on non-discriminatory and multilaterally agreed rules and procedures consistent with international trade law and practices. In this context, open and free international trade in forest products should be facilitated.

(b) Reduction or removal of tariff barriers and impediments to the provision of better market access and better prices for higher value-added forest products and their local processing should be encouraged to enable producer countries to better conserve and manage their renewable forest resources.

(c) Incorporation of environmental costs and benefits into market forces and mechanisms, in order to achieve forest conservation and sustainable development, should be encouraged both domestically and internationally.

(d) forest conservation and sustainable development policies should be integrated with economic, trade and other relevant policies.

(e) Fiscal, trade, industrial, transportation and other policies and practices that may lead to forest degradation should be avoided. Adequate policies, aimed at management, conservation and sustainable development of forests, including, where appropriate, incentives, should be encouraged.

14. Unilateral measures, incompatible with international obligations or agreements, to restrict and/or ban international trade in timber or other forest products should be removed or avoided, in order to attain long-term sustainable forest management.

15. Pollutants, particularly air-borne pollutants, including those responsible for acidic deposition, that are harmful to the health of forest ecosystems at the local, national, regional and global levels should be controlled.

Bibliography

A Global Poverty Trap (1996), *The Economist* 20-26 July,1996, p 52

Adams WM. (1990), ***Green Development: Environment and Sustainability in the Third World***, Routledge, London.

Alexander Kiss and Dinah Shelton (1991), ***International Environmental Law***, Transnational Publishers Inc., London.

Allen, Robert (1980), ***How to Save the World,*** Barnes and Noble Books, Totowa, New Jersey.

Andrew Hurrell and Benedict Kingsbury (Ed) (1992), ***International Politics of the Environment***, Clarendon Press, Oxford.

Anil Markandya and Julie Richardson (Eds.) 1992, ***Environmental Economics,*** Earthscan, London.

Ball, Simon and Bell, Stuart (1995), ***Environmental Law,*** Blackstone Press Ltd., London.

Barbier, Edward B(1987), The Concept of Sustainable Economic Development, ***Environment Conservation*** 14(2)) pp 101-110.

Bernaeur, Thomas (1995), The Effect of International Environmental Institutions: How We Might Learn More, ***International Organisation,*** 49, 2 Spring 1995, pp 351-377.

Blumm, Michael C (1992), ***Environmental Law,*** Dartmouth, Aldershot.

Boyle, Alan E.(1991), Saving the World? Implementation and Enforcements of International Environmental Law Through International Institutions, ***Journal of Environmental Law*** , Vol.3, No. 2, pp 229-245.

Breton, Tony (1994), ***The Greening Michavelli***, Earthscan, London.

Broad, Robin *et al* (1996), Whither the North-South gap ? ***Third World Quarterly***, Vol.17 No.1, pp 7-17, 1996.

Bromley DW (1991), ***Environment and Economy***, Blackwell, Oxford, UK.

Brown *et al* (1987), ***Global Sustainability: Toward Definition,*** Environment Management 11(6) pp 713-719.

Brown, Lester R *et al* (1994), ***Vital Signs 1994,1995.,*** World Watch Institute, Earthscan, London.

Chichilmisky, Graciela (1996), Undervaluing The Earth, ***New Economy***, Summer 1996, Vol. 3 issue 2 pp.15-19.

Common, Michael (1995), ***Sustainability and Policy,*** Cambridge University Press, Cambridge.

Dommen, Edward (Ed) 1993, ***Fair Principles for Sustainable Development***, UNCTAD, Edward Elgar, England.

Economic Growth (1996), ***The Economist,*** 25-31 May, 1996, pp 25-26.

Field, Bary C.(1994), ***Environmental Economics***, McGraw-Hill Inc. New York.

Fikret Berkes (Ed) 1989, ***Common Property Resources***, Belhaven Press, London.

Gilpin, Alan (1996), ***Dictionary of Environment and Sustainable Development***, John Wilky & Sons, New York.

Gosovic, Branislav (1992), ***The Quest for World Environmental Co-operation***, Routledge, London.

Grubb, Michael (1995), Seeking For Weather: Ethics and the International Debate on Climate Change, ***International Affairs,*** 71, 3 (1995), pp 463-496.

Gundling, Lothar (1990), Our Responsibility to Future Generations, ***The American Journal of International Law***, Vol.84,1990, pp 207-212

Harris, Stuart (1996) Economics of the Environment: A Survey, ***The Economic Record*** , Vol.72 No. 217, June 1996, pp 154-171.

Iftikar Ahmad and Jacobus A. Dodeman (Eds.), 1995, ***Beyond Rio,*** ILO Studies Series, Macmillan, London.

Imber, Mark (1993), Too Many Cooks? The Post-Rio Reform of the United Nations, ***International Affairs,*** 69, I (1993), pp 55-70.

Ken Conga (1995), Greening the United Nations: Environmental Organisations and the United Nations System, ***The Third World Quarterly,*** Vol.16, No. 3, 1995, pp 441-455.

Krishna Prasad Oli (1996), Legal Instruments for Sustainable Environmental Management in Nepal, ***Environment and History.*** 2 ,1996, pp 231-248.

Lenihan, John *et.al.* (Eds.), 1979, ***Environment and Man,*** Vol. Ten, Blackie, Glasgow and London.

Mahbub Ul Haq *et al* (Ed) 1995, ***The UN and the Bretton Woods Institutions,*** Macmillan, London.

Malcolm, Rosalind (19940, ***A Guide Book to Environmental Law,*** Sweet & Maxwell, London.

Meadows, Donella H *et al* (1972), ***The Limits to Growth,*** Earthscan, London

Meadows, Donella H *et al* (1992), ***Beyond the Limits,*** Earthscan, London

Nagendra Singh (1987), Foreword to ***Environmental Protection and Sustainable Development,*** WCED, 1987, pp i-xxi.

Our Common Future, WCED, 1987, Oxford University Press, Oxford.

Pearce DW and Warford JJ (1993), ***World Without End,*** World Bank.

Pezzey, John (1989), ***Economic Analysis of Sustainable Growth and Sustainable Development,*** World Bank.

Princern, Thomas and Finger, Mathias, 1994, ***Environmental NGOs in World Politics,*** Routledge, London.

Redclift, Michael(1987), ***Sustainable Development,*** Routledge, London.

Rivilin, Benjamin (1995), Development Dilemmas and Tensions at the UN, ***International Social Science Journal*** 143, March 1995, UNESCO.

Runge, Carlisle Ford (1986), Common Property and Collective Action in Economic Development, ***World Development***, Vol.14., No. 5, 1986, pp 623-635.

Sands, Phillippe (1995), ***Principles of International Environmental Law***, Vol.1, Manchester University Press, New York.

Sjostedt, Gunnar (1993), (Ed) ***International Environmental Negotiations***, Sage Publications, London.

Solow RM.(1991), ***Sustainability: An Economist's Perspective,*** in Robert Dorfman and Nancy S Dorfman (Eds.), *Economics of the Environment,* W W Norton & Company, New York, 1993, pp 179-187.

Stokke, Olav (Ed) 1991, ***Sustainable Development***, p 114 Frank Cass-London.

Susskind L. and Ozawan (1992), Negotiating More Effective International Agreements in Hurrell. A. and Kingsbury. B (Eds.), ***The International Politics of the Environment.*** Oxford, Clarendon.

Talbot, Lea M (1984), ***The World Conservation Strategy,*** University of New England, England.

Tonn, Bruce E(1988), Philosophical Aspects of 500 Years Planning, ***Environment Planning,*** A.20.

Tromans, Stephen (1992), International Law and UNCED, ***Journal of Environmental Law,*** Vol.4, No.2, 1992, pp 189-202

Turner R K, Pearce D, and Bateman I, (1994), ***Environmental Economics,*** Harvester, Wheatsheaf, New York.

UN Chronicle, June 1992, p 63

UN Year(s) 1968, 70, 72, 82, 87, 90, & 92.

Vogler, John and Imber, Mark F.(Ed) (1996), ***The Environment and International Co-operation***, Routledge, London.

Wade, Robert (1988), ***Village Republics,*** Cambridge University Press, Cambridge.

Weiss E.B (1990), What Obligation does Our Generation Owe to the Next? ***The American Journal of International Law,*** Vol.84, 1990, pp 190-207.

William J Baumol and Wallace E Oates(1979), ***Economic Environmental Policy, and the Quality of Life,*** Prentice-Hall Inc, England

Winter, Gerd (1989), Perspectives for Environmental Law-Entering the Fourth Phase, ***Journal of Environmental Law,*** Vol.I.No.1.,1989

World Bank (1992), ***World Development Report 1992***

World Bank (1994), ***Making Development Sustainable,*** Washington DC